P9-CRK-259

Garden Designs

SIMPLE STEPS TO
BEAUTIFUL FLOWER GARDENS

TIME-LIFE BOOKS, ALEXANDRIA, VIRGINIA

TIME LIFE

HOW-TO

Garden Designs

Introduction

You can begin your garden projects months before the weather permits you to work outdoors. During the cold winter months, gardening catalogs start to arrive, filling the eye with visions of how wonderful your garden might look throughout the coming seasons. Your local library will have gardening books and magazines—useful sources of information and fresh ideas. You may also want to talk with other gardeners and visit local garden centers to find out which plants are best suited to your area.

In this book you will learn about color, design, and what makes a garden succeed. It will show you how to lay out entirely new gardens, perhaps by adding a rose arbor or a showy border in front of stately evergreens. You will also learn how to spruce up your established beds; for instance, by tucking spring bulbs in among your ground cover or adding an edging of brightly colored annuals to accent an existing shrub bed.

Easy-to-follow design ideas and planting tips simplify garden planning. Throughout the growing season you will find this book a useful reference, filled with information on when and how to perform routine garden chores. Try recording your garden ideas and plans in a notebook. You can sketch the layout of your present garden and note where you would like to add plants, or try one of our suggested garden designs for a fresh new look. The pages that follow will help you transform your winter dreams into the reality of a beautifully designed and maintained garden. ❧

Getting Started

Designing and planting a new garden is an exciting undertaking. Chances are you've already been admiring a neighbor's attractive yard, noting favorite plants in nurseries and catalogs, or imagining how a garden might look in different locations on your property.

You can start off in the best possible way by analyzing the needs of your particular garden site. Knowing your soil's characteristics and what you can expect from it is the first step toward a successful garden. Awareness of rainwater drainage patterns will help prevent costly planting mistakes, as will familiarity with the amounts and locations of the sun and shade your property receives. Putting in some thought and planning time beforehand will help to ensure that you choose the right plants for your garden.

In this section, you'll learn that appropriate gardening tools can make a difference in how smoothly your project runs. You'll find out which tools you're most likely to need, what to look for when choosing them, and how to keep them in top shape. As you fill your garden planner with information and ideas, include a budget for the gardening tools you'll need. Your careful planning will be amply rewarded as you work in your garden and as it matures. ❧

Testing Your Soil

JAR TEST

Identifying your soil type is the first step in determining what amendments should be added to your garden. Soil is composed of minerals, organic material, living organisms, air, and water, all of which are important to plant growth. Soil types are based on the percentages of different sizes of mineral (rock) particles. From largest to smallest, these particles are sand, silt, and clay.

Soils with a large percentage of sand are called coarse-textured or light and allow water to pass through them quickly. These soils have little ability to retain moisture so they dry out rapidly at the surface, and any nutrients present are easily washed away. Clay soils are fine-textured and heavy. They retain water and plant nutrients well but are slow to drain in spring and compact easily. Soils with a large percentage of silt are intermediate in their ability to retain water and nutrients.

Soil also contains organic material, or humus. Organic matter allows in more air and helps to retain moisture. It also provides nutrients essential for healthy plant growth. Although there is no such thing as perfect soil, high organic matter content combined with a mix of approximately one-third each of sand, silt, and clay is desired.

To determine soil type, follow the steps at right, then measure the depth of each level in the jar. The stratification will give you the approximate soil composition. ❧

HAVE ON HAND:

▶ Clean garden trowel
▶ Clean plastic pail
▶ Newspapers
▶ Rolling pin
▶ Clean quart jar with lid
▶ Nonsudsing dishwasher detergent
▶ Water
▶ Watch
▶ Grease pencil
▶ Ruler

Dig 6 holes 6 inches deep, 8 feet apart. Remove a ½-inch-wide soil strip from each; place in pail, mix.

Spread on newspaper to dry. Cover with paper, roll with pin to pulverize soil. Place 1 cup of soil in jar.

Add 1 teaspoon detergent, 2 cups water. Shake for 1 minute; let settle 1 minute. Mark top of sand layer.

In 2 hours, mark silt layer above sand. In 2 days, or when water is clear, mark clay layer above silt.

pH TEST

This test determines the pH, or acidity, of your soil. Some soil nutrients become unavailable to plants at certain pH levels. Test pH before adding amendments so you will add the right amounts. Easy-to-use pH test kits are available at garden centers and by mail order. Or, you can have your soil tested by your state Cooperative Extension Service.

The scale for measuring pH ranges from 1.0 to 14.0, with neutral at the center (7.0). A number below neutral indicates acidic soil; a number above 7.0 indicates alkaline soil.

Most plants prefer soil in the pH range between 6.0 and 7.5, but certain plants need either acidic or alkaline soil. If you live in an area with high rainfall, the soil is probably acidic. If wild azaleas and mountain laurel are common, it may be very acidic. If you live in a dry region, the soil is probably alkaline. Abundant native sage, bass-wood, or bush cinquefoil will all confirm the presence of alkaline soil.

If necessary, your soil pH can be altered. Lime, crushed oyster shells, hardwood ashes, manure, and bone-meal will sweeten acidic soil. Sulfur, sawdust, pine needles, or composted leaves can be used to lower the pH if your soil is too alkaline.

Efforts to raise or lower pH can be affected by your soil type. Sandy soils need lower amendment amounts than clays, silts, or loams do. If your soil is high in organic matter, it may need more amendments, since organic matter buffers chemical changes.

To raise the pH by one point on sandy soils, add 1 to 2 pounds of lime per 100 square feet; to lower the pH by one point, incorporate 2 to 3 pounds of sulfur. For clays, silts, or loams, you will need 5 to 6 pounds of lime or 4 to 5 pounds of sulfur for each 100 square feet.

Fill a clean test tube from your purchased soil pH test kit ¼ full of dry garden soil.

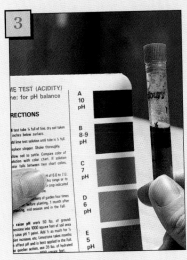

Add lime test solution until test tube is ½ full (or up to marked line). Close tube, shake thoroughly.

Allow contents to settle. After the liquid clears, compare its color to the chart supplied with kit.

Determine the amount of lime or sulfur needed to raise or lower your soil pH to the desired level.

Determining Sun and Shade

Understanding your plants' light preferences and determining whether you have full sun, partial or indirect sun, full shade, or partial shade are important to the success of your garden. Direct or full sun is equivalent to a minimum of 6 to 8 hours a day, usually during the hottest hours. If a site gets 4 to 6 hours with some early or late-day sun, it is considered partial sun. Partial shade means dappled sunlight or up to 2 hours of direct sunlight very early or late in the day. It is equivalent to indirect sun—sites that are bright even though they get no direct sunlight. Complete or full shade means no direct sunlight and little reflected light.

Providing the right amount of sun or shade need not be an exacting exercise since many plants tolerate a range of conditions. Climate and rainfall can also influence sun or shade requirements. In cool, moist regions, shade-loving plants will stand more sun than in hot, sunny, dry climates. In hot areas, even plants that prefer full sun may benefit from afternoon shade. Shade changes with the seasons as well. In northern regions there are dramatic differences in spring, summer, and fall. Plants located in spring shade may end up in summer sun as the sun moves more directly overhead. Shade-loving perennials can usually tolerate full sun in spring. Under deciduous trees, for example, the less intense, direct spring sun warms soil and gets shade-loving perennials off to a quick start.

When you can't locate shade gardens under trees or to the north side of buildings, use other garden features, such as a trellis, framed lattice, overhead pergola, nearby hedgerow, or fence, to provide shade for all or part of a garden. Simple solutions, like placing short, shade plants in the shadow of tall, sun-loving ones, can be used in sunny spots. ❧

HAVE ON HAND:

▶ Graph paper

▶ Regular pencil

▶ Compass

▶ Watch

▶ Tape measure (50 foot)

▶ Four colored pencils

▶ Permanent black marker

Accurately measure and draw your garden to scale on graph paper. Use a compass to locate North and mark it on your paper for orientation.

Outline overlapping areas for different hours this way: full shade—4 colors, part shade—3 colors, partial sun—1 or 2 colors, full sun—no color.

Mark the position of shade-casting features (trees, buildings, hills, fences). Check for accuracy before drawing with permanent marker.

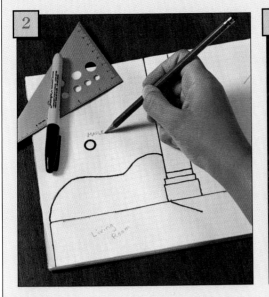

On a sunny day, visit your garden at 2-hour intervals (10:00, noon, 2:00, and 4:00). Measure and sketch in shadow locations each time.

Repeat process in 3 months using a new sheet of paper to determine seasonal changes in your yard's sun and shade patterns. Date map.

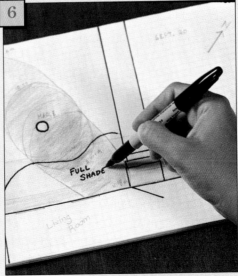

Use maps to plan your garden, matching plant choices to sun or shade areas. Add features to provide additional shade, if desired.

HERE'S HOW

READING WEEDS

Using a reference book, identify three or four of the most prevalent perennial weeds in your garden area. Use perennial species because, unlike annuals, they must survive year after year in the same soil. If they are thriving, your garden's conditions meet their specific needs. Compare reference information about each species. You should find similar conditions where these weeds grow, such as a sunny, well-drained site. This is a quick, reliable way to identify your garden's general soil type and moisture content as well as sunlight exposure.

Understanding Drainage

Garden drainage refers to the rate at which soil allows water to pass through it, or percolate. You can get a general idea of which areas in your yard have poor drainage by noting where puddles remain after a heavy rain (often in the lowest spots). Except in the driest climates, it's better to site gardens in areas slightly higher than the surrounding land so surface water drains away easily.

Drainage is greatly influenced by soil type. Gravelly or sandy soils allow surface water to infiltrate quickly, and so are very well drained. Heavier soils, clays and silts, tend to hold water on the surface longer; if water actually puddles,

soil is poorly drained. If your soil test showed a good mix (see Testing Your Soil, page 8) of sand, silt, and clay, your soil is probably well drained.

Conditions below the surface, however, may make your soil drain differently from what your soil test would lead you to expect. Topsoil spread over gravel will drain well even if it contains a fair amount of clay. Shallow bedrock, limestone formations, or hardpan—a layer of dense material underlying the topsoil that inhibits drainage—may be present. Whatever type of soil exists over such barriers will tend to have poor drainage.

Soil drainage can be improved by incorporating organic matter such as compost, leaf mold, or well-rotted manure. Soil that drains too quickly requires frequent watering to keep plants from drying out and to replenish nutrients because they leach out rapidly. Adding organic matter will improve the soil's ability to retain both moisture and nutrients. In heavy clays and silts, compost helps loosen and aerate the soil, allowing water to drain through more quickly and reducing the soil's tendency to compact. For soils that drain slowly, you may wish to create raised beds to provide better drainage for all but the most moisture-loving plants. ✿

Test drainage on a sunny day when garden soil is relatively dry. Squeeze a handful of soil; it should not form a sticky, compact, solid clump.

One by one, fill each hole to the top with water. Immediately after filling the hole, note the exact time and depth of water.

HAVE ON HAND:

▶ Shovel

▶ Hose

▶ Yardstick

▶ Water

▶ Watch

▶ Paper

▶ Marker

Examine your yard for possible low spots or areas where soil type changes. Test these and potential garden sites before you plant.

In midmorning or later, dig 2 to 4 flat-bottomed holes at least 1 foot deep and spaced evenly over potential garden sites.

Record the water depth in each hole every 15 minutes for 1 hour. Soils with adequate drainage lose approximately 1 inch per hour.

Note which test sites meet this requirement, and which are faster or slower. Plan to amend any soils that drain much more rapidly or slowly.

HERE'S HOW

REPLACING LOST NUTRIENTS

Excess water can leach nutrients from garden soil, resulting in conditions similar to poorly fertilized soil. Check plant growth and color for clues to which nutrients might be missing. Plants low in nitrogen (N) have yellowish foliage and are stunted. In phosphorus (P) deficient soils, lower plant leaves turn a reddish purple color and roots are stunted. Low potassium (K) results in few flowers, stunted or weak growth, and yellow-spotted or marked leaves with brown, burnt edges. When the weather is dry, add a balanced fertilizer (5-10-10) for phosphorus or potassium deficiencies by scratching it into the soil surface in the recommended amounts. Use 10-10-10 for nitrogen deficiencies in your soil.

Working with Garden Tools

CHOOSING TOOLS

Good-quality garden tools are a gardener's best investment. Although they cost more at the outset, reliable, long-lasting tools will pay their way in the long run. If you choose carefully, you can save money by buying only the tools and tool features you really need.

Look for tools with metal that is heavy gauge. Blades should be free of nicks and have smooth, sharp edges. Since a tool's weakest point is where the blade and handle meet, blade extensions should completely envelop wooden handles, without an open break. The best handles are made of hickory or ash, or high-strength fiberglass. Movable parts should work freely and smoothly, without grinding. Ask about the availability of replacement parts.

If possible, give tools a trial run before you purchase them. You are looking not only for utility and longevity in a tool but also for how comfortably you can use it. Check to make certain the tool you are buying is the proper size and weight for you. Tools should fit your hand size and arm length as well as your height and strength. They should also fit your right or left hand, depending on which hand you routinely use. Heavy blades should be balanced by long handles for leverage, stability, and maneuverability. ❧

CLEANING TOOLS

Keep your garden tools clean and you will extend their life; keep them working their best and you will help prevent the spread of infection and disease in the garden. Quick cleanups after each use and at the end of the gardening season won't take much time and will ensure that your garden implements will be ready for use the next time you need them.

Each time you use your tools, remove clinging or caked-on soil with a hose or brush. Tools without motors can be rinsed with water as long as metal parts are well dried to prevent rust. Cutting-tool blades on hoes, spades, shovels, forks, rakes, and edgers should be cleaned to remove soil, plant debris, and/or sap. After hosing, dry the tools thoroughly and rub blades with a clean, oily rag to keep them corrosion-free. Inspect tools for nicked or bent blades and replace those where necessary.

Wipe down tool handles and check for splits, cracks, or splinters; replace handles that are badly damaged. Sand handles lightly to smooth out splinters and rough spots. As a preventative measure, when you purchase tools, coat the wooden handles with clear varnish to protect the wood and help keep them like new. Touch up the protective varnish whenever necessary. ❦

HAVE ON HAND:

▶ Water

▶ Wire brush

▶ Clean rags

▶ Lightweight oil

▶ Stiff bristle brush

▶ Soap

▶ Sandpaper

▶ Clear varnish and brush

METAL SURFACES. *Rinse with water and scrub with wire brush if necessary. Dry thoroughly.*

Coat metal with lightweight oil. Work oil into joints of moving parts. Check directions for motors.

WOODEN SURFACES. *Clean with stiff brush, soap, and water. Dry thoroughly.*

Sand splinters, touch up with clear varnish. Replace badly cracked or split handles for safety.

KEEPING LARGE TOOLS SHARP

Keep your large tools sharp and you will reap important benefits. Sharp tools are easier and safer to work with since they are less likely to slip, jam, or balk. Dull blades are more likely to tear plants, leaving them susceptible to disease and insect damage; sharp blades make clean cuts, reducing chances of infection.

Cutting tools are prone to a number of mishaps. Stony or compacted soils dull hoes, fork tines, spades, and shovels.

Even dropping a tool on a hard surface can bend or nick it enough to make a difference in its performance. Keep your tools in top condition by keeping them clean, dry, and oiled, and by replacing damaged parts. Also, use tools only to do the work for which they were designed. Misuse can dull blades, bend parts, and loosen joints.

Make a habit of resharpening tool blades after each use or during big jobs as they dull. Use a vise to hold them securely and sharpen them properly. For example, sharpen a hoe on the face of the blade, the side toward you as you work. Otherwise, slicing through soil and weeds will be like trying to cut with the wrong side of a knife. Always wear safety glasses, and keep a first-aid kit close at hand, just in case.

Sharpening a mower blade is more complicated than it looks. You may want to learn from a professional before tackling the job yourself. 🌿

HAVE ON HAND:

- ▶ Safety glasses
- ▶ Wire brush
- ▶ Vise
- ▶ Metal file
- ▶ Clean rag
- ▶ Lightweight oil

Wearing safety glasses, use a wire brush to remove all dirt and rust from metal blades.

Check the angle of the existing beveled edge. Clamp the tool securely into a vise.

Using a metal file, file away from yourself at the existing angle of bevel until the blade is sharp.

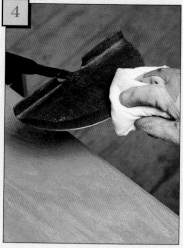

Wipe clean. Coat blade surface with a lightweight oil to protect it from rust. Store tool in a dry place.

STORING TOOLS

Tools need a spot where they will be easily accessible yet not in your way. Locate them where you can find individual tools quickly and return them easily to their designated spots.

Tools placed in their proper locations also have less chance of being damaged. By contrast, tools repeatedly left outdoors may not be salvageable after rust and weathering have taken their toll. (An occasional lapse won't hurt if handles are revarnished and metal surfaces sprayed with oil or silicone prior to storage for the winter.)

HAVE ON HAND:

▶ Pegboard, if desired

▶ Wall or pegboard hooks

▶ Tape measure

▶ Black marker

▶ Masking tape for labels

An empty wall in a dry barn, garage, or shed is an ideal place for large tools. Be sure hardware, such as nails, pegboard hooks, rack fasteners, or dowels, is secure. Always hang tools with blades toward the wall to prevent injury. Push corks over sharp tines before hanging tools. Place short items such as bagged materials and watering cans beneath hanging tools where you won't trip over them. A glance at an organized tool area should let you find what you need quickly and tell you if something is missing.

Small tools will be easy to replace if their outlines have been drawn where they are to be hung. They can also be stored in easily lifted, see-through containers put on shelves out of the reach of children. Covered jars or small, multiple-drawer tool chests provide storage for such small items as nails. List contents on containers to help you find specific items. 🌿

Use wall in dry area or install a pegboard against wall. Lay tools on the floor in front, as they will be hung.

Determine spacing and number of hooks needed to hang each tool securely. Place hooks.

Hang tools on hooks; adjust so that handles and blades don't overlap. Label each spot, or outline tool.

Place watering cans and bagged materials below the hanging tools, for safety and easy access.

A Guide to Garden Tools

DIGGING

Look for well-balanced tools with smooth handles made from fiberglass, ash, or hickory and heavy-gauge metal blades extending from long, solid collars.

SPADE
Sharp, rectangular blade with front-rolled step at top attached to long and straight or short D-shaped wooden or fiberglass handle. Use for edging, transplanting, cutting, and removing sod.

HAND TROWEL
Scoop-shaped, 6-8-inch-long, forged, heavy-gauge metal blade balanced with well-anchored wooden or cushioned plastic handle.

CUTTING

Tools should be made from high quality, heavy-gauge metal with replaceable parts and cushioned grips. Check for balance. Safety locks should release easily.

PRUNING SHEARS
Curved bypass blades hold stem in place while blades cut like scissors. Buy heavy-gauge, replaceable metal blades. For stems up to ¾ inch.

LOPPING SHEARS
Curved blades attached to 12-28-inch wooden or fiberglass handles cushioned with rubber shock absorber. Larger blades should have longer handles for leverage and balance. For stems up to 1¾ inches.

MAINTENANCE

Choose tools with one-piece, heavy-gauge metal blades with continuous collars solidly attached to smooth, strong handles. Check that they fit your strength and size.

GARDEN CART
Constructed of plastic, metal, fiberglass, or wood with large tires. Various sizes. Should have removable back panel for dumping. Needs more room to turn than wheelbarrow but is more stable.

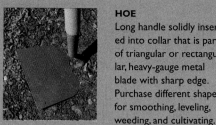

HOE
Long handle solidly inserted into collar that is part of triangular or rectangular, heavy-gauge metal blade with sharp edge. Purchase different shapes for smoothing, leveling, weeding, and cultivating.

Special Tools

Some tools will become indispensable, saving you money and time. Good examples are soaker hoses and garden carts. Others are expensive investments, used only once or twice a year. You may decide to rent a rototiller, for example, instead of buying, or to share ownership with family, a friend, or a neighbor. 🌿

Soaker hoses are porous rubber hoses that allow water seepage. In climates with high evaporation rates, savings in money and watering time are substantial. Buy hoses with end caps to prevent clogging by soil. Be careful when cultivating nearby.

GARDEN FORK
8-inch-wide head with 1-foot-long steel tines. Long and straight or short D-shaped handle. Use for turning compost, breaking up or aerating soil, lifting and dividing perennials.

ROUND-POINT SHOVEL
Rounded, heavy-gauge, sharp metal blade with rolled-step top, long and straight or D-shaped handle. Arched collar provides best leverage and lift. Use to dig holes, move soil, and plant and transplant.

METAL GARDEN RAKE
Comb-like, heavy-gauge metal head, 2- or 3-inch tines. Look for one-piece head, forged construction, sturdy collar, long handle for good leverage. Use for debris and to level, smooth, and tamp.

GRASS SHEARS
Long, sharp, scissorlike blades with reinforcing spring and heavy-gauge metal squeeze handles. Use to shear annuals and trim grass along garden walk or stone edging.

GARDEN SCISSORS
Sharp, heavy-gauge metal scissors with reinforced handles. Useful for cutting flowers, deadheading plants, trimming foliage, and removing seed pods.

ASPARAGUS FORK
12-18-inch heavy-gauge metal shank with sharp, V-notched head in thick, wooden or cushioned plastic handle. Useful for removing weeds with long taproots and root-pruning.

HAND CULTIVATOR
Three- or four-clawed, heavy-gauge metal head. Use for hand-weeding around established plants. Also useful for cultivating, aerating soil, and breaking up soil lumps.

HOSE
Pliable ⅝- or ¾-inch diameter, reinforced, 4-ply rubber hose for watering. Choose hoses with an internal pressure rating of 500 PSI and brass couplings for durability.

STEEL LAWN RAKE
Variable head widths, heavy-gauge, flexible steel tines, bent tips. Look for spring-braced head, secure attachment to long, sturdy handle. Use to prevent injury to shallow-rooted or brittle-stemmed plants.

Hose nozzles change water patterns and reduce or increase pressure. Durable, heavy-gauge plastic or metal nozzles with adjustable heads are preferable. Cushioned, insulated squeeze grips can be locked in ON position. Nozzles should come apart easily for cleaning.

Rototillers need careful research. Investigate different ones as to vibration, maneuverability, and whether size is suitable for your garden jobs. Rear-tine tillers work best for deep cultivation but may be too large for small gardens. Look for adjustable handlebars, quality construction, accessories, and a good warranty.

Preparing Your Planting Bed

Preparing your planting bed may not be the most exciting part of accomplishing your garden design, but it is one of the most important parts of gardening. The time and energy you spend to ensure that your soil is cultivated and amended properly can save you countless hours of weeding, cultivating, and amending later. Loose, crumbly soil with good fertility and drainage is the perfect place for strong root systems to grow. Preparing your garden bed is your chance to provide the best permanent setting for a garden that will thrive for years to come.

Cultivating at the right time will recruit nature to help in the preparation of your garden bed. If you dig your new bed in the fall, repeated freezing and thawing will work to break up the soil, making your job easier in the spring. Digging when the soil is ideally moist—neither too wet nor too dry—will also save unnecessary effort on your part.

Soil improvement and cultivation go hand in hand. Balancing pH, improving drainage, and increasing fertility will mean you can grow a wide range of plants. The following pages will show you the methods to use and materials you need to set the stage for any number of garden designs. ❧

Cutting a New Bed from Lawn

Once you've decided where you want your new garden to be, chances are good that some of your lawn will need to be removed in order to accommodate your plans.

If you are planning ahead, fall is the best time to create a new garden bed, enabling you to plant as early in spring as the soil can be worked, and allowing soil amendments time to become incorporated. But spring is fine, too. You will be successful in either season if you follow the simple steps outlined here.

First, be certain that disturbing the soil will not also disturb your underground sprinkler system, if you have one. Move or adjust it for your new bed as necessary. Before you dig, check the soil in the proposed garden. It should be moist, not wet, when you dig. If you are laying out a large garden, check the weather forecast to make sure you will have sufficient time to complete the job. A rainy day can make wet sod and soil heavy and unworkable.

Don't be tempted to rototill lawn grass into a new garden. Even poor grass will take on new life when turned under with intact roots. Remove sod and add it to your compost pile for the future. Spread a thick layer of compost or other organic matter and a sprinkling of fertilizer (following application rates on label) over the area, digging them in at least 1 foot deep to create a rich, well-drained garden bed. 🌸

HAVE ON HAND:

▶ Stakes

▶ String

▶ Hammer

▶ Garden hose

▶ Lime

▶ Spade

▶ Garden cart

Outline straight sides with stakes and string. Use hose to outline curves and mark perimeter with lime.

Use spade to dig straight down at boundary. Insert blade 6 inches and dig around garden perimeter.

Working in rows, dig 4 inches down, slide spade under grass and lift sod. Cut ends again, if needed; lift strip.

Shake sod strip over soil to remove loose topsoil. Place discarded sod into garden cart to be composted.

Cultivating Your Soil

SIMPLE DIGGING

The best garden soil is loose and easy to work. A simple, or single, dig—when soil is dug to a depth of approximately 1 foot—can help you achieve better soil. Simple digs are recommended for sandy, light soil, annual gardens (where plants are replaced each spring), and to begin gardens for shallow-rooted shrubs and perennials. Such plants do not need soil that is deeply cultivated, but they do need rich, loose soil in order to perform well.

Single digs add compost or other amendments to the upper topsoil. When mixed into the soil's surface, nutrients become available to shallow-rooted plants. Compost or other organic matter will also help your garden retain moisture, reducing the need for frequent watering.

Don't exhaust yourself unnecessarily by digging when your soil is too wet or too dry. Wet soil is heavy and will stick to your shovel and other garden tools. Dry soil can have the consistency of concrete. Check the soil for proper moisture levels and either wait or water before starting to dig.

If you choose to begin your new bed in the fall, stifle weed growth by spreading black plastic over the entire garden. Cover the plastic with mulch to hide it for the winter, then use the mulch to give your new garden a boost when it's time to plant in the spring. 🌺

HAVE ON HAND:

- ▶ Stakes
- ▶ String
- ▶ Hammer
- ▶ Round-point shovel
- ▶ Garden cart or wheelbarrow
- ▶ Soil amendments
- ▶ Garden fork
- ▶ Garden rake

In garden area with sod removed, mark a 2-foot-wide row the width of garden with stakes and string.

Use shovel to dig trench 8 to 12 inches deep. Transfer soil to cart. Mark next trench, dig to 8 to 12 inches.

Place soil in empty trench as you dig. Add amendments. Use fork to break clumps, mix. Continue until end.

For the last trench, use soil from first trench, mix in amendments. Level and smooth with rake.

Cultivating Your Soil

DOUBLE DIGGING

Double digging means loosening the soil deeper than the 1-foot (one shovelful) depth of a simple dig, making this method the most appropriate preparation for permanent, deep-rooted plants, such as most perennials and shrubs. Since they may remain undisturbed for many years, these plants need deeply cultivated soil to accommodate the extensive root systems or long taproots they will grow. Soil that is loosened and enriched with nutrients from the start will give your plants the conditions they need to thrive.

To prepare an area with long grasses or mature weeds for a double dig, first clip heads that have gone to seed. If seeds are dispersed over your garden area, they can germinate over a long period of time—sometimes more than 20 years. Put clippings into a paper bag and discard them. This simple trick will save you much of the work of intensive cultivation for seasons to come. After seeds are disposed of, mow or cut back remaining plants before removing sod.

When you dig a bed or planting hole, add the appropriate soil amendments for your plants. Read the description of the soil your plant grows best in and then compare it to the soil where you are planting. A soil test will enable you to do this (see Testing Your Soil, page 8). You may need to make your soil more alkaline with agricultural lime or more acidic with sulfur. Also, add nutrients, ideally from organic material (which also improves soil texture) rather than from chemical sources (see Here's How, page 27). 🌸

HAVE ON HAND:

- ▶ Garden spade
- ▶ Round-point shovel
- ▶ Yardstick
- ▶ Stakes
- ▶ String
- ▶ Hammer
- ▶ Garden cart or wheelbarrow
- ▶ Garden fork
- ▶ Soil amendments
- ▶ Garden rake

With spade, remove sod in area to be cultivated. Measure a 2-foot-wide trench across the width at one end. Mark with stakes and string.

Measure and mark next trench. Remove soil 8 to 12 inches deep; place it in first trench. Add amendments. Go to second trench and Step 3.

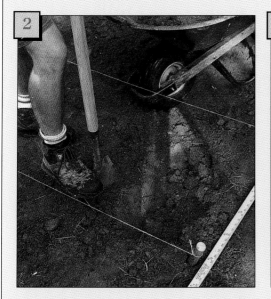

Use a round-point shovel or garden spade to dig the trench 8 to 12 inches deep. Remove the soil, putting it in a garden cart or wheelbarrow.

Insert fork tines completely into soil at bottom of trench. Turn soil over and break up clumps. Add amendments to the soil and mix well.

HERE'S HOW

PREVENT DIGGING INJURY

Lifting a fork, shovel, or spade the wrong way can interrupt your gardening career. Spend more time in the garden and less on the injured list by learning to dig correctly.

Keeping the tool vertical, use one foot and the weight of your body to push it deeply into the soil. Then angle the tool in order to scoop up the earth. When lifting a load, bend your knees, separate your hands on the tool handle for the best leverage, and straighten bent knees, lifting with your legs and not your back. Keep your back as vertical as possible when lifting. Doing this will help you avoid unnecessary strain on your back muscles, where you are most vulnerable.

Continue for entire length of bed, filling trenches with topsoil from adjacent ones, loosening bottom soil and adding and mixing amendments.

Use the soil in your garden cart from the first trench to fill the last trench. Level and smooth the entire planting area with a rake.

Improving Your Soil

In order to grow vigorously, plants need the proper amounts of sun, water, and air. They also need appropriate nutrients and compatible chemical balances in the soil. Adding the right soil amendments to make sure your soil is in the best shape possible will ensure your garden's success.

Your soil can be improved in three basic ways. You can improve its texture, its nutrients, and its content. Which of these you do will depend upon the special characteristics of your soil.

Amendments such as peat moss and builder's sand increase water-holding capacity or improve drainage. Compost, ground-up wood, and limestone change soil texture, add nutrients and adjust the pH (acid or alkaline) levels. Often, a particular amendment will do more than one job. Compost, for example, not only adds nutrients but also improves the texture of your soil.

Test pH and nutrient level of soil. Obtain needed quantities of amendments recommended for type of soil and amount to be improved.

You can test your soil's nutrient content and pH level with a home kit available from local garden centers or by sending a soil sample to your state Cooperative Extension Service (see Testing Your Soil, page 8). With results in hand, you can match your soil to the plants you want to grow. For example, should you choose rhododendrons and discover that your soil is alkaline, you can lower the soil pH by adding sulfur. If you like peonies and find that your soil is acidic, you will need to add limestone to the soil because peonies require a high pH. A soil pH of from 6.0 to 7.0, however, is fine for a wide range of garden plants.

Amendments can be added to new or existing gardens in the spring or fall. They can also be added to established gardens up until midsummer, after which plants should be left alone to prepare themselves for winter.

HAVE ON HAND:

▶ Soil testing kit

▶ Soil amendments

▶ Round-point shovel

▶ Garden rake or cultivator

▶ Spreader or trowel

▶ Garden fork or rototiller

▶ Water

NEW BED. Use a garden fork or a rototiller to mix the amendments thoroughly and deeply into the loosened soil.

Prepare new planting bed (see Cultivating Your Soil, page 23). In established garden, use a rake or cultivator to loosen soil between plants.

Spread appropriate amendments evenly over loosened soil using a shovel for fertilizers, a spreader or trowel for lime or sulfur.

ESTABLISHED BED. Rake amendments into the soil or use a cultivator to work between plants. Avoid injuring stems or roots.

ALL BEDS. Smooth soil-bed surface with garden rake. Water the soil thoroughly to settle soil and activate amendments.

HERE'S HOW
FAST AND EASY COMPOSTING

Compost is a dark, rich, crumbly organic material with a coarse texture. You can create it out of many things you might ordinarily throw away.

To make a compost bin, fasten together the ends of a 10-foot piece of 3-foot-high, 14-gauge wire mesh. Place 2 to 4 inches of leaves, grass clippings, vegetable and fruit scraps from your kitchen, and plant litter from undiseased plants (but no meat, pet waste, or anything containing fats) into cylinder.

Add a 2-inch layer of topsoil and another 2 inches of manure if available. Alternate layers. Water pile and keep moist for a week. On the eighth day, remove the wire cage and set it beside the pile. Fork the material back into the wire cage and water again. Repeat the process until you can no longer distinguish the various ingredients and its dark, crumbly appearance tells you that the compost is ready for use.

A Guide to Soil Improvement

ADDING NUTRIENTS

Most organic materials add nutrients while improving soil texture and composition. Shop for the best price; check for bulk availability for large areas.

BONEMEAL
Finely ground, white or light grayish, rendered slaughterhouse bones. Bonemeal adds nitrogen and phosphorous to the soil. May attract animals.

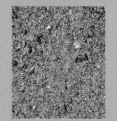

LEAF MOLD
Decomposed or partly decomposed leaves and plant litter, usually dark brown in color. Light, earthy odor. Slowly releases nutrients into the soil, especially phosphorus. Also useful as a mulch.

IMPROVING TEXTURE

Heavy soils need improved aeration and drainage while light, sandy soils need improved water retention and structure. Learn your soil type before amending.

COMPOST
Improves aeration and compaction in heavy soils; increases water retention in sandy soils. Also improves soil structure in all soil types and keeps nutrients from being washed away.

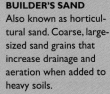

BUILDER'S SAND
Also known as horticultural sand. Coarse, large-sized sand grains that increase drainage and aeration when added to heavy soils.

ADJUSTING pH

Most soils need some pH adjustment so that nutrients are available to plants. Change pH slowly, and check nutrient levels at regular intervals.

SOIL SULFUR
Yellow powder; lowers high pH levels in soil by acidifying it. Use on a windless day; work sulfur immediately into soil. Can cause skin irritation. May burn plant leaves in sun.

GROUND LIMESTONE
White powder or granulated pellets of calcium carbonate; will slowly lower the acidity of soil. Apply in the fall and retest pH level in the spring.

Special Supplements

Thick seeding of specific plants, called green manures or cover crops, is an effective, relatively inexpensive way to add organic matter and nutrients—especially nitrogen—to your soil. These plants can hold soil during the winter, smother weeds, and encourage soil-enriching earthworm activity. A month before planting your garden, till them into the soil where they will continue to work, retaining water and adding nutrients. 🌿

BUCKWHEAT. *Quick to germinate and fast to grow, it covers the soil completely, choking out even perennial weeds. Sow in spring or summer. Turn buckwheat under as soon as it begins to blossom. Adds organic matter.*

WELL-ROTTED MANURE
Also known as composted cow manure. Available as an odorless, dried amendment Use aged manure only. Incorporate into soil before midsummer for extra nutrients.

COMPOST
Decomposed organic material, usually deep brown in color with an earthy odor. Use as a mulch and incorporate into the soil for slow-release nutrients.

FISH EMULSION
Liquid, concentrated, fisheries by-product with distinct fishy odor. Source of nitrogen. Can be diluted and sprayed onto plants or the ground. May attract animals.

PERLITE
White, heat-expanded, lava rock that lightens soils by increasing drainage and aeration. Excellent in soil mixes for containers and as rooting medium. May look unattractive in garden soils.

VERMICULITE
Heat-expanded mica. Light, flaky, soft, gray or white soil amendment, rooting medium, and mulch. Vermiculite improves drainage and soil aeration. May look unattractive in garden soils.

WATER RETENTION POLYMER CRYSTALS
Granules combine with water to form gel. Slow release eliminates need to water frequently; reduces transplant shock. Most biodegradable; can remain effective up to five years.

SAWDUST
Increases soil acidity. Fresh sawdust heats when decomposing; buy last year's product or let sit for a year before using. Heat can injure or kill plants and rob soil of nitrogen.

OYSTER SHELLS
Calcium carbonate from coarsely ground oyster shells. Use as you would use lime. Allow 6 months before retesting soil for pH change. Aim for ½ point increase per year with either amendment.

HARDWOOD ASHES
Ashes from burned hardwoods lower soil acidity and add potassium. Incorporate only cooled ashes, especially in established beds. Can burn plants if applied too heavily.

ANNUAL RYEGRASS. *Plant at the end of the growing season to control soil loss. Killed by cold temperatures, it will form a protective winter mat over the soil surface. Turn under in the spring to add organic matter.*

LEGUMES. *Beans, peas, clover, and vetch add nitrogen and organic matter to soils. Turn beans and peas grown for green manure under after vegetables are harvested. Water retention is significantly improved in sandy soils.*

Designing for All Seasons

Part of the fun and reward of gardening is planning your garden for all-season interest. With your notebook (or camera) in hand, you can sketch, describe, and record plants that catch your interest in each season. Then replicate or adapt the projects and plant suggestions you will find on the following pages for your own attractive, year-round garden.

As you plan your design, use season-extending tricks of the trade. For instance, you can plant later-emerging plants or ground covers to camouflage fading spring bulb foliage. Or use a colorful annual bed to create a new garden every year. Take the opportunity to experiment with color, height, texture, and unusual plant varieties.

Know the mature size of the plants in your garden and resist the temptation to overplant at the outset. Your carefully planned design will hold its shape much better in seasons to come if you fill in a new perennial bed or border with bulbs and annuals until the permanent plants reach their mature size.

Don't feel you have to plant an entire garden for each season if you want year-round interest in one bed. A scattering of fall or winter plants in a summer bed or border will be enough to extend the season. If you want to do more, include bulbs for spring and fall, evergreen shrubs or shrubs with colorful winter stems, and perennials that have unusual seed pods for attention-getting beds and borders throughout the year. ❧

Delicate Spring Wildflowers

THIS GARDEN THRIVES WITH

SUN
Full

WATER
Medium

SOIL
Average, well drained

Wildflower gardens have gained popularity in part due to their reliable, beautiful blooms year after year. The fact that this type of garden is easy to care for is an added incentive for you to begin your own. Choose flowers native to your region, where they have already adapted to the climatic conditions. You will find volunteer plants springing up during subsequent years.

These gardens can be as small as a patch in your yard or as large as a meadow. Small plots are the most manageable, allowing you to try scaled-down experiments with new plants and different combinations. Adding new wildflowers will make your garden more diverse, but avoid aggressive species as they may choke out other plants. When purchasing plants, buy from reputable nurseries that propagate from their own stock. Digging wild plants can destroy an entire colony, and the survival rate for removed plants is very low. It is also illegal to dig up any endangered wild species.

Wildflowers are attractive to wildlife. You will find butterflies and pollinating bees frequenting your garden, and birds will come for the seeds and insects. There's no better introduction to the workings of the natural world than this special kind of garden.

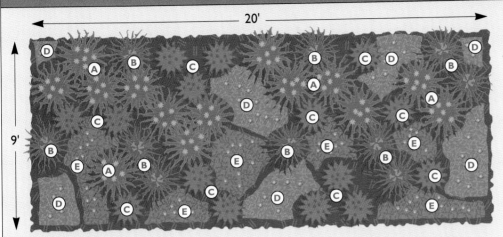

PLANT LIST

A. Wallflower, 14 yellow, 2 to 2½ feet tall

B. Beard-tongue, 10, 2 to 5 feet tall

C. Bachelor's-button, 15, 2 to 2½ feet tall

D. Corn poppy, 1 to 3 seed packets, 1 to 3 feet tall

E. California poppy, 1 to 3 seed packets, 1 to 2 feet tall

(See next page for more on plants.)

1. Mark an area 9 x 20 feet. Remove sod, till soil, add 1 to 2 inches of compost, and retill the soil.

2. Rake the surface smooth so that the areas without plants will be prepared as a seedbed for the poppies.

3. One foot from the back, beginning 2 feet from the left side, plant 1 wallflower (A), 1 beard-tongue (B), 2 bachelor's-buttons (C), then 1 wallflower, 1 beard-tongue, 1 bachelor's-button. Plant 1 beard-tongue 2 feet from the right side.

4. Offset the second row beginning on the left side. Plant 3 wallflowers and 1 bachelor's-button. Leave a 4-foot space, then plant 2 wallflowers. Leave another 4-foot space, then plant 1 wallflower and 1 beard-tongue.

5. Offset the third row from the left, planting 2 bachelor's-buttons and 2 wallflowers. Leave a 4-foot space, then plant 1 bachelor's-button, 1 wallflower, 1 bachelor's-button, and 1 wallflower.

6. For the fourth row, offset beginning at left border, planting 1 beard-tongue. Leave a 4-foot space, then plant 1 beard-tongue and 1 wallflower. Leave a 4-foot space, then plant 1 beard-tongue. Leave another 4-foot space, then plant another beard-tongue.

7. Offset the fifth row, beginning 4 feet from the left side, planting 1 wallflower, 1 beard-tongue, 1 bachelor's-button. Leave a 6-foot space, then plant 1 bachelor's-button, 1 beard-tongue, and 1 more bachelor's-button.

8. Offset row six, beginning 5 feet from left side: plant 1 bachelor's-button; leave a 4-foot space, then plant 1 more bachelor's-button; leave a 4-foot space, then plant 2 bachelor's-buttons.

9. Mulch around plants and water them well.

10. Mark poppy (D) and (E) areas. Mix poppy seeds with finely pulverized soil or clean sand, then sprinkle on marked areas. Pat soil to ensure seed/soil contact. Do not cover with soil: seeds need light to germinate. Water lightly.

HERE'S HOW

HARVESTING WILDFLOWER SEEDS

Cut plants at the end of a sunny day. Place a paper bag around each seed head and secure with a rubber band. Hang plants upside down in a shaded, low humidity area. When seeds are dry, separate by shaking on a screen with mesh large enough to permit the seeds to pass through. Store in an airtight container in the refrigerator.

Delicate Flowers for Spring Beauty

This mostly annual garden begins to flower in the spring and continues blooming well into the summer. For a continued easy-care garden, leave some flowers in place to produce seeds so the plants can self-sow. You may also choose to harvest your wildflower seeds (see Here's How, page 33) for planting later or starting from seed indoors.

Choose a well-drained area that receives full sun all day. Because the plants described here are either natives or have naturalized, they do not need soil amendments or special care. However, adding compost as a mulch will reduce the need to water, help the plants to become established more quickly, and decrease competition from weeds.

As you expand your wildflower garden, you can add to its natural look by continuing to mix plants and randomly scatter various kinds of native seeds.

WALLFLOWER
Cheiranthus cheiri
2-2½ feet tall
Zones 4-9
Orange, yellow, red, or brown, 1-inch flowers in clusters April to June; 3-inch, lance-shaped leaves; average to rich, well-drained soil; full sun; medium water. Biennial treated as annual. Self-sows.

BEARD-TONGUE
Penstemon barbatus
2-5 feet tall
Zones 4-10
Pink, tubular, 3-inch flowers in upright clusters May to August; lance-shaped leaves along stems; average, well-drained soil; full sun; medium water. Short-lived perennial treated as annual. Self-sows.

BACHELOR'S-BUTTON (CORNFLOWER)
Centaurea cyanus
2-2½ feet tall
All zones
Deep blue, fluffy flowers on wiry stems May to August; gray-green, lance-shaped leaves; average, well-drained soil; full sun; medium water. Prolific bloomer; attracts wildlife. Good cut flower. Self-sows.

CORN POPPY (SHIRLEY POPPY)
Papaver rhoeas
1-3 feet tall
All zones
Silky, 2- to 3-inch, cup-shaped flowers in shades of red May to September; deeply cut, hairy leaves; average, well-drained soil; full sun; medium water. Self-sows.

CALIFORNIA POPPY
Eschscholzia californica
1-2 feet tall
All zones
Orange to yellow, cup-shaped flowers March to August; deeply cut, blue-green foliage; average, well-drained soil; full sun; medium water. Birds eat seeds. Self-sows.

CARE FOR YOUR WILDFLOWER GARDEN

SPRING Carefully remove winter mulch without disturbing new seedlings. Remove weeds. Thin and transplant seedlings to stand 1 foot apart. Add new annuals. Mulch garden lightly as seedlings grow taller and the plants fill in.

SUMMER Water garden during dry periods. Remove spent flowers to promote continuous bloom but allow seed pods to form late in the season for self-sown plants the following spring. Cultivate soil between plants; mulch to retain moisture.

FALL After the first killing frost, remove dead annuals. With your mower set on the highest setting, mow remaining plants. Shake dried seeds into the garden area. Use healthy plant debris as a mulch to hold wildflower seeds in place during the winter.

Alternative

BOLD WILDFLOWERS

Choose less delicate-looking wildflowers for a garden where summers are hot and dry. In the prairie regions, where drying winds and erratic moisture challenge most plants, beautiful prairie wildflowers survive with minimal care. These rugged and mostly perennial plants have adapted by spreading underground in locations where seeds have difficulty reaching through a thick mat of grasses to the soil. They easily adapt to a variety of growing conditions and will give you a spectacular, natural-looking garden.

Emphasize the striking reds and yellows in your wildflower garden by mixing in the gray-green foliage and blue flowers of pitcher sage. The smaller blanket flower and the more graceful gayfeather will contrast with the larger plants. Coarse-textured sunflowers and coneflowers should be placed toward the back of the garden where they will have space to grow and won't overpower other plants.

Beside a patio or at the edge of your yard, prairie wildflowers can be part of a sophisticated planting or provide a transition from your garden into the natural landscape. These hardy plants will need plenty of space to grow and require little care.

PRAIRIE CONEFLOWER
Ratibida pinnata
3-4 feet tall
Zones 4-9
Yellow, 2-inch, daisy-like flowers with dark, raised centers, July to September; deeply cut, dark green, coarse leaves; average to poor, well-drained soil; full sun; low to medium water. Tolerates dry soils and drought.

MAXIMILIAN SUNFLOWER
Helianthus maximiliani
5-10 feet tall
Zones 5-10
Golden yellow, 3- to 4-inch, daisy-like flowers with a deeper yellow center, August to October; large, oval, serrated green leaves; average, well-drained soil; full sun; low to medium water. Tolerates dry soil and drought. Birds eat the seeds.

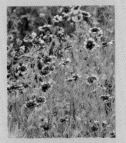

BLANKET-FLOWER
Gaillardia x grandiflora 'Dazzler'
1-2½ feet tall
Zones 2-8
Deep red with yellow borders, 2- to 3-inch, daisy-like flowers with dark red centers, April to October; gray-green, lance-shaped, hairy, coarse foliage; average to poor, well-drained soil; full sun; medium to low water. Tolerates heat, dry soil, and drought.

GAYFEATHER (BLAZING STAR)
Liatris spicata
2-4 feet tall
Zones 3-10
Feathery, pinkish purple flowers on wand-like, upright stems, July to September, above low foliage forming a clump; average, well-drained soil; full sun; medium to low water. Flowers attract butterflies. Long-lasting cut flower.

PITCHER SAGE
Salvia azurea
3-5 feet tall
Zones 5-10
Azure blue, slender, arching flower spikes, August to October; gray-green, coarse, lance-shaped leaves; poor to average, well-drained soil; full sun; low to medium water. Tolerates heat and drought. Good cut flower. Attractive to bees and butterflies.

A Spring Bulb Garden

THIS GARDEN THRIVES WITH

SUN
Full to part

WATER
Medium

SOIL
Average to rich

Celebrate winter's end with the bright, welcoming colors of a spring bulb garden. Bulb gardens are daily indications of spring's progress, from the emergence of the first shoots to the opening of colorful blooms. For best results, choose bulbs that will perform well in your climate. In all climates, tulips will give the best show if new bulbs are planted each year.

Your spring bulb garden can be either geometric or free form in shape. As you are planning a bulb garden, lay it out with string and stakes or mark the area with lime to be certain the scale is appropriate for the surrounding landscape. A small garden may seem lost in a vast lawn area, for example, but can look spectacular located at the edge of your yard or near the entrance to your house. A large garden may need some space around it to have the most impact.

Locate your spring bulb garden where you will be able to enjoy watching its progress. Bulbs usually make their best show in large masses of a single color or drifts featuring a minimum of six to twelve bulbs. Keep this rule of thumb in mind in the fall as you prepare and plant for your spring color display.

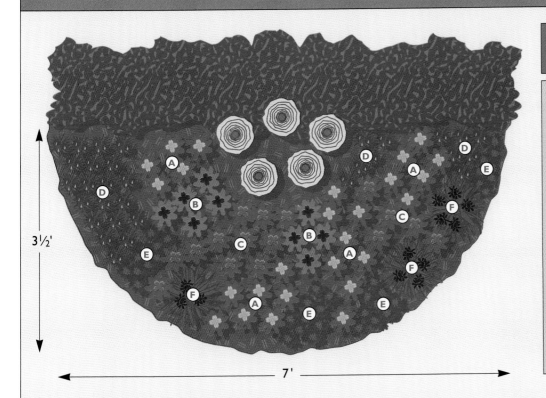

3½'

7'

PLANT LIST

A. Darwin tulip, 26 yellow,
   20 to 24 inches tall

B. May-flowering tulip, 9 maroon,
   18 to 30 inches tall

C. Lily-flowered tulip, 16 pink,
   20 to 24 inches tall

D. Dutch iris, 31 blue, 2 feet tall

E. Grape hyacinth, 37 blue,
   6 to 12 inches tall

F. Spanish bluebell, 3 blue,
   12 to 20 inches tall

(See next page for more on plants.)

1. In early fall, mark the edge of a half circle garden along a woodland border. Remove sod, taking care not to damage tree roots.

2. Mark bulb areas with lime. Lay bulbs on the ground in each area, spaced approximately as follows: tulips and iris 4 to 6 inches apart, bluebells 1 foot, and grape hyacinths 3 inches.

3. Use a bulb planter or shovel to dig holes for bulbs. Mix bulb fertilizer with soil at bottom of each hole, following directions on package label. Plant 5 yellow tulips (A) beginning in back and left of half circle center. Plant 5 maroon tulips (B), 11 pink tulips (C), 4 maroon tulips, 8 yellow tulips, 5 pink tulips, 5 iris (D), and 6 yellow tulips as you move from left to right, as shown.

4. Beginning at left again, plant 20 iris and 10 grape hyacinths (E) next to the iris.

5. Plant 1 bluebell (F), 7 yellow tulips, and 10 grape hyacinths in the front of the garden.

6. Continue on the right side with 9 grape hyacinths, 2 bluebells, and 6 iris. Plant 8 grape hyacinths along the edge next to the iris.

7. Water thoroughly and mulch the entire garden with 1 to 3 inches of light, organic mulch—preferably with shredded leaves from the overhead trees.

HERE'S HOW

USING A BULB PLANTER

To minimize disturbance to the tree or shrub roots nearby, use a convenient bulb planter. Push the bulb planter into the soil to the appropriate depth, then pull it back up. Place a single tulip bulb or 2 or 3 smaller bulbs in the bottom of the hole and reinsert the bulb planter. Squeeze the handle or tap to replace the soil plug. Firm the ground surface.

Colorful Spring Bulbs

Popular spring bulbs, such as tulips, produce beautiful flowers in a wide range of colors, including bicolors. Plant a wide mix of tulips or combine them with other spring flowering bulbs, such as grape hyacinths or bluebells, for contrast or to extend the bloom period.

Overplanting with perennials, low-growing evergreens, or ferns will help retain soil moisture in warmer climates. The spring-flowering bulbs will grow up through the foliage of these other plants. Later, the yellowing bulb foliage will be hidden by perennial leaves.

In warm climates, place tulip bulbs in the refrigerator (40° to 50° F) for six to eight weeks prior to planting. In cold climates, plant hardy bulbs in early fall. Follow directions for recommended amounts of fertilizer and planting depths for the types of bulbs you are planting. ❧

DARWIN TULIP
Tulipa 'Golden Apeldoorn'
20-24 inches tall
Zones 3-8
Large, yellow, cup-shaped flowers from April to May; succulent, blue-green basal leaves with flower stalk rising from center; average to sandy, well-drained soil; full/part sun; medium water.

MAY-FLOWERING TULIP
Tulipa 'Queen of Night'
18-30 inches tall
Zones 3-8
Deep purplish maroon, cup-shaped flowers on long, sturdy stems in May; 3 or 4 succulent, green basal leaves with flower stalk rising from center; average to sandy, well-drained soil; full/part sun; medium water. Good cut flower.

LILY-FLOWERED TULIP
Tulipa 'Queen of Bartigon'
20-24 inches tall
Zones 3-8
Pink, recurved petals on vase-shaped flowers in May; succulent, blue-green basal leaves with flower stalk rising from the center; average to sandy, well-drained soil; full/part sun; medium water.

DUTCH IRIS
Iris xiphium 'Wedgwood'
2 feet tall
Zones 5-10
Large, blue flowers April to May, sometimes with yellow or orange on falls; grass-like leaves; average, moist, well-drained soil; full/part sun; medium water. Good cut flower.

SPANISH BLUEBELL (WOOD HYACINTH)
Endymion hispanicus 'Excelsior'
6-12 inches tall
Zones 5-9
Deep blue, bell-shaped flowers May to June; strap-shaped, green leaves; average to rich, moist soil; part sun/shade; medium to high water.

GRAPE HYACINTH
Muscari botryoides
12-20 inches tall
Zones 6-12
Clusters of small, blue, tubular flowers April to May; dark green, grass-like leaves; average, well-drained soil; full/part shade; medium water.

CARE FOR YOUR SPRING BULB GARDEN

SPRING Mulch garden with compost after removing wire mesh and mulch installed in the fall. During dry weather, water regularly. Remove flowers as they fade.

SUMMER Remove seed heads from tulips and iris, but do not cut down foliage until completely yellow. Cut grape hyacinths back when foliage is yellow. Remove pods on bluebells.

FALL In cold regions, cover garden with a non-compacting mulch and pine boughs. Protect bulbs from animals by covering with small-grid wire mesh tucked 6 inches into soil. ❧

Alternative

A COLORFUL COMBINATION GARDEN

Planting bulbs with similarly colored perennials can create arresting combinations of flowers and foliage. Use early flowering perennials, such as sweet violets and columbine, with spring-flowering bulbs, such as tulips and hyacinths, for striking flower displays of color, form, and scent.

Select plants with foliage and flower colors that combine well. With the richly shaded colors of purple violets, for example, use the bicolored 'Arabian Mystery' triumph tulip described at right. Or try something a little unusual, such as feathery parrot tulips to offset the violet's heart-shaped foliage. Tulips are available in a wide range of shapes, sizes, and with different bloom times. Experiment to find your favorites.

Spring-flowering bulbs, especially hyacinths, can also be fragrant. Cool spring temperatures may mask their scent so cut some blossoms to take indoors where warmer temperatures will enhance their perfume. Combine fragrant hyacinths with other low-growing flowers in shades of purple, perhaps creeping phlox, for a sweetly scented combination garden. ✿

TRIUMPH TULIP
Tulipa '**Arabian Mystery**'
12-18 inches tall
Zones 3-8
Deep reddish purple petals with ivory edges on cup-shaped flowers April to early May; succulent, green basal leaves with flower stalk rising from center; average to sandy, well-drained soil enriched with compost; full/part sun; medium water. Good cut flower.

SIBERIAN IRIS
Iris sibirica
24-30 inches tall
Zones 3-9
Deep violet-purple blooms on tall stems from May through June; strap-like, dark green leaves; average, well-drained soil; full sun; medium water.

HYACINTH
Hyacinthus orientalis '**Blue Jacket**'
8-10 inches tall
Zones 4-8
Dense spikes of fragrant, blue-purple blossoms from March to May; succulent, dark green basal leaves; average, well-drained soil; full sun; medium water. Good cut flower.

SWEET VIOLET
Viola odorata
4-8 inches tall
Zones 4-8
Deep violet-blue, sweet-scented blossoms April to May; rounded or heart-shaped, deep green leaves form a 4- to 8-inch mound; average, moist, well-drained soil enriched with compost; full/part sun; medium water. Attractive ground cover after blooming.

COLUMBINE
Aquilegia '**Dragonfly Hybrids**'
18-22 inches tall
Zones 4-8
Long-spurred blooms in various shades of blue, purple, yellow, red, and bicolors from May through June; delicate, fern-like foliage; average, well-drained soil; full sun; medium water.

Vibrant Summer-into-Fall Color

THIS GARDEN THRIVES WITH

SUN — Full

WATER — Low

SOIL — Poor to average

This home's setting provided the inspiration for a vibrant border offering color from early summer into the fall. If your location is hot and sunny, this plan could work for you. Heat-loving plants screen sunny windows, offering shade as well as a garden view. Here, the informal, cottage style of the house is complemented by easy-care, old-fashioned plants.

Look at colors in and around your home to help determine the colors to use in your garden. Here, white trim on windows and fence is echoed in the cleome and summer savory, while spirited colors are offset by dark siding on the house. Note how the pink cosmos at the back separates the white of the window trim from the tall, white cleome blossoms. The dark green cleome foliage provides a backdrop for the carpet of yellow, pink, and orange along the stone walk.

Keep in mind when planting that dark or bold hues tend to draw more attention than paler hues, and that tall plants draw more attention than short ones. Balance your border by placing short, bold-colored flowers near the front and tall plants with large, light-colored flowers at the back. You can tone down large, imposing plants by placing plants with small, delicate foliage nearby.

14'

14'

PLANT LIST

A. Cosmos, 17 pink, 4 to 5 feet tall

B. Cleome, 10 white, 4 to 5 feet tall

C. African marigold, 15 yellow,
2 to 3 feet tall

D. Chrysanthemum, 5 pink,
2 feet tall

E. Summer savory, 12 white,
12 to 18 inches tall

F. Zinnia, 20 orange,
14 inches tall

(See next page for more on plants.)

HERE'S HOW

LAYING OUT A QUARTER-CIRCLE GARDEN

Mark back corner and front edge boundaries with three stakes. Attach a 14-foot-long string to the back corner stake. With string pulled tightly, walk in an arc between the other two stakes while marking the pattern on the ground with lime. Dig sod from the curve first to keep the pattern from being distorted.

1. In spring after all danger of frost, mark off a 14-foot, quarter-circle garden (see Here's How). Remove sod, till soil, and spread a 3- to 4-inch layer of compost over area.

2. Plant 17 cosmos (A) 1 foot apart in the back left corner.

3. Plant 10 cleome (B) 2 feet apart, in a staggered row ending in the upper right corner.

4. Plant marigolds (C) 2 feet apart. Start with row of 6 from left edge of garden, then offset 2 more rows, one of 4 and one of 5, in front of first row.

5. Plant 5 chrysanthemums (D) 2 feet apart, to right of marigolds and 1 foot in front of cleome, coming forward as shown.

6. Plant 12 summer savories (E) 8 inches apart, in offset rows of 3, as shown.

7. Complete your planting with a grouping of 20 zinnias (F) 1 foot apart. Extend along front of border to meet the summer savories.

8. Mulch entire garden and water plants thoroughly.

Colorful, Long-Lasting Flowers

The plants in this striking border are heat-loving and will tolerate dry conditions. You'll find them easy to grow, requiring little maintenance other than occasional watering in extended dry periods.

These annuals are self-sowing, meaning that they will provide volunteer plants for your garden in the coming years. At the end of the season, simply leave some faded blossoms to form seed pods. Let the mature pods winter in the garden, and watch for seedlings in the spring.

Extend the enjoyment of your border by planning for fragrance, cut flowers, and culinary uses. Here, the aromatic summer savory planted along the stone walkway will release a hint of perfume when grazed. Summer savory will also provide a bounty of leaves for tea and seasoning. And most of the plants in this border are delightful as cut flowers. 🌺

COSMOS
Cosmos bipinnatus 'Imperial Pink'
4-5 feet tall
All zones
Deep rose-pink flowers on sturdy branches all summer; airy, fine foliage; poor to average, well-drained soil; full sun; low water. Water only when dry. Stake where windy.

CLEOME (SPIDER FLOWER)
Cleome hasslerana 'Helen Campbell'
4-5 feet tall
All zones
White petals, protruding stamens, rounded flower heads open from bottom up June to frost; aromatic leaves; poor to average, well-drained soil; full sun; low water. Water when dry.

AFRICAN MARIGOLD (AZTEC MARIGOLD)
Tagetes erecta 'Diamond Jubilee'
2-3 feet tall
All zones
Lemon yellow flowers until frost; deeply cut leaves; average, well-drained soil; full sun; low water. Water when dry. Overfeeding creates leaves, few blossoms.

CHRYSANTHEMUM
Chrysanthemum x morifolium
2 feet tall
Zones 5-10
Flat, double, orchid pink blooms July to frost; dense, deeply cut, aromatic foliage; average, well-drained soil; full sun; low water. Water when dry.

SUMMER SAVORY
Satureja hortensis
12-18 inches tall
All zones
Small, lavender or white flowers July through August; narrow, shiny, aromatic leaves; average to rich, well-drained soil; full sun; low water. Use leaves in foods or herbal teas.

ZINNIA
Zinnia angustifolia 'Star Orange'
14 inches tall
All zones
Orange, daisy-like blooms until frost; narrow leaves; average, well-drained soil; full sun; low water. Water in the morning if dry.

CARE FOR YOUR VIBRANT SUMMER-INTO-FALL BORDER

SPRING In early spring, remove the winter mulch, taking care not to disturb any newly sprouted seedlings. Apply a light layer of compost mulch as seedlings grow taller and your plants begin to fill in.

SUMMER In windy areas, stake taller plants. During long, dry periods, water plants deeply. Remove faded blossoms to encourage more blooms, and trim plants that are too aggressive. Late in the summer, allow selected seed pods to form.

FALL After the first frost, shake dry seed pods over the soil to dislodge any seeds that have not yet fallen. Place a covering of mulch, such as chopped leaves, on your garden for the winter to protect the seeds from wind and temperature fluctuations. 🌺

Alternative

DRAMATIC PLANTS FOR A SUMMER-INTO-FALL GARDEN

If the architectural style of your home is modern, you can complement it by substituting some of the plants listed here in your summer-into-fall garden. Nurseries offer new plants as well as unique shapes, new flowers, and bold colors for old favorites. Check your local nursery.

Substituting plants can change not only the style but also the maintenance of your border, so choose carefully to satisfy your garden conditions. The alternatives offered here will thrive in dry, well-drained soils, but consider other factors as well. For example, locate plants that can withstand some abuse along a walkway. Lamb's ears is not only drought tolerant, but its soft, fuzzy texture invites handling by old and young alike—and it's sturdy enough to withstand an occasional trounce. A quick snip will remove crushed and torn leaves with no damage overall.

Prolong flowering by deadheading, or removing spent blossoms. Also, consider cutting flowers while at their prime for drying. Blanket-flower and the blossoms from lamb's ears are good choices. As fall arrives, gazanias can be dug up, potted, and brought indoors for continuing color during the cold winter months. 🌼

BLANKET-FLOWER
Gaillardia pulchella **'Gaiety Mix'**
2 feet tall
All zones
Nearly round flowers up to 3 inches wide in yellow, maroon, orange, or rose all summer until frost; poor or sandy to average, well-drained soil; full sun; low water. Heat tolerant; water only during drought. Remove faded blossoms for continued flower production.

MEXICAN SUNFLOWER
Tithonia rotundifolia **'Yellow Torch'**
4-6 feet tall
All zones
Yellow, daisy-like 3- to 5-inch flowers with a raised yellow center, all summer until frost; velvety, deep green, heart-shaped leaves; dry, well-drained soil; full sun; low water. Water only during drought. Remove faded blossoms for continued flower production. Long-lasting cut flowers.

SUMMER POINSETTIA (FOUNDATION PLANT)
Amaranthus tricolor salicifolius **'Early Splendor'**
30-36 inches tall
All zones
Tiny flowers among leaves; plant grown mainly for foliage, 6- to 8-inch, large, coarse leaves in deep maroon topped by brilliant fuchsia foliage; poor to average, well-drained soil; full sun; low water. Water only when dry.

GAZANIA (TREASURE FLOWER)
Gazania rigens **'Sundance'**
1 foot tall
All zones
Daisy-like, 3- to 4-inch flowers all summer in shades of gold, red, orange, pink, bicolored stripes or rings; grows from central rosette of deeply lobed, silvery, hairy foliage; average, well-drained soil; full sun; low water. Water only during drought. Remove faded blossoms for continuous flowering.

LAMB'S EARS (WOOLLY BETONY)
Stachys byzantina
18 inches tall
Zones 4-8
Tiny, deep pink flowers among raised, woolly flower stalks June through August; low-growing, silvery blue, woolly foliage, 1 foot high; poor to average, well-drained soil; full sun; low water. Water only during drought.

A Sizzling-Hot Summer Border

THIS GARDEN THRIVES WITH

SUN
Full

WATER
Medium

SOIL
Average

The garden at left will provide you with color all summer long. These striking annual flowers in dramatic reds, lemony yellows, candy pinks, and rich purple-violets typify bright, sun-drenched summer days.

Locate your border along a wall, a fence, or in front of a shrub border where it will receive full sun all day. During the summer, when the sun is most direct, the colors will seem especially brilliant.

Place foliage plants in groups to form a background for bright colors and between strong colors as a buffer. Here, the dusty miller's silver foliage offsets the deep red of the geraniums and tones down the visual impact of neighboring yellow marigolds.

Keep similar colors together, rather than separating groups or scattering plants throughout the garden, for a bolder effect. The strongest colors, such as the geranium's red, are kept to the front, and darker colors, such as the salvia's purple-violet, serve as a backdrop. You can incorporate your own favorite summer flowers and colors for long-lasting summer sizzle.

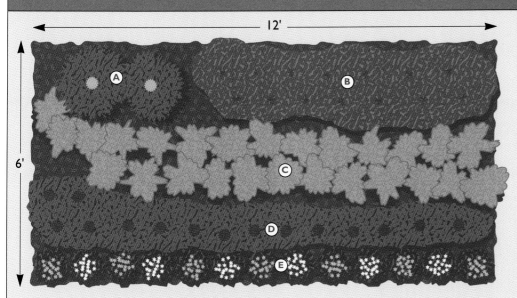

PLANT LIST

A. African marigold, 2 yellow,
2 to 3 feet tall

B. Salvia, 14 purple,
20 to 24 inches tall

C. Dusty miller, 26,
20 to 24 inches tall

D. Geranium, 15 red,
12 to 18 inches tall

E. Sweet alyssum, 6 pink, 7 white,
4 to 6 inches tall

(See next page for more on plants.)

1. Measure an area 12 x 6 feet; remove sod and stones. Till soil 1 foot deep. Spread 4 inches of organic compost over the surface and till the soil again, 4 to 6 inches deep.

2. Beginning at the back left side of your border, plant 2 yellow marigolds (A) 2 feet apart, 18 inches from the back.

3. To the right of marigolds, 1 foot from the back, plant 2 rows, each with 7 salvia (B). Leave 1 foot between plants. Stagger the rows.

4. Plant a row of 13 dusty millers (C) 3 feet from the back of the border, 1 foot apart. Stagger a second row of 12 in front of first row. Plant 1 dusty miller 1 foot behind back row on the far left.

5. In front of the dusty millers plant 13 red geraniums (D) 1 foot apart. On the left behind this row, plant 2 red geraniums as shown.

6. In front of the row of geraniums, plant 1 row of 13 sweet alyssum (E), with plants 1 foot apart. Alternate pink and white plants, as shown.

7. Mulch your entire garden with a layer of organic mulch, such as compost or chopped leaves; water well.

HERE'S HOW

TAKE CUTTINGS FROM YOUR GERANIUMS

With a clean, sharp knife, cut 4- to 6-inch stems from healthy geranium plants. Remove flower buds and leaves on lower 2 inches. Push cuttings into sterile, well-drained growing medium. Water, and place container in a sunny, east window. Water every 3 or 4 days. Check for rooting with a light tug after 2 weeks. Cuttings are ready to replant when you encounter resistance.

Hot-Colored Summer Blooms

Annuals are at peak performance during the hot summer months. The annuals in this garden will thrive all season with minimal care. In addition, marigolds, salvia, and dusty millers are good cutting plants, and sweet alyssum will reward passersby with its pleasant scent.

One of the tricks of the trade when planting is to remove all flower buds and pinch back the terminal stem (the growing tip). This begins a process that forces side branches to develop lower on the stem, giving you bushy plant growth and more flower heads. For even denser growth, pinch back again when plants are between one-half and two-thirds their mature height.

The plants featured here are great performers during hot weather, but take care not to let your soil become hard and overly dry. Lightly cultivate the soil surface between plants to allow water to infiltrate and reach the roots. 🌺

AFRICAN MARIGOLD
Tagetes erecta 'First Lady'
2-3 feet tall
All zones
Bright yellow, 4- to 6-inch flowers all summer; finely cut, aromatic foliage; average, well-drained soil; full sun; low water. Performs well in hot weather. Good for cutting.

SALVIA
Salvia splendens 'Atropurpurea'
20-24 inches tall
All zones
Purple-violet flower spikes above foliage all summer; oval leaves; average, well-drained soil; full sun; low water. Withstands cool temperatures.

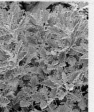

DUSTY MILLER
Senecio cineraria
20-24 inches tall
All zones
Insignificant yellow-white flowers; velvety, stiff, finely cut, silvery white foliage; average, well-drained soil; full sun/light partial shade; low water. Withstands cool fall temperatures.

GERANIUM
Pelargonium x hortorum 'Sprinter Scarlet'
12-18 inches tall
All zones
Red flower clusters all summer; lobed, rounded leaves may be red-tinged; average, well-drained soil; full sun/light shade; low water.

SWEET ALYSSUM
Lobularia maritima 'Easter Basket'
4-6 inches tall
All zones
Scented, white, pink, or lilac flower clusters all summer; mounding foliage; average, well-drained soil; full sun/light shade; low water. Shear after bloom for regrowth.

CARE FOR YOUR SIZZLING HOT SUMMER BORDER

SPRING Pinch back flower heads and terminal stems on your plants for bushy growth and abundant flowers. Mulch your garden with organic materials to provide essential nutrients and smother weeds.

SUMMER Water well during extended periods of dry weather, and keep sufficient mulch over the soil to retain moisture. Deadhead to keep your plants tidy and encourage more blooms on annuals.

FALL Prior to frost, take cuttings from geraniums to winter over for next year. After killing frost, remove and compost healthy plant debris. Dispose of diseased materials away from garden area; do not compost. 🌺

Alternative

A COOL, CALM, DROUGHT-RESISTANT SUMMER BORDER

If you would rather have a border that is relaxing and soothing, a planting of pastel colors will convey a refreshing mood. Pale blues, lavenders, greens, and whites are part of the cool-color spectrum that is associated with serenity. Plants with pale yellow blooms blend well with the cooler hues and add a bit of sunshine.

Delicate as they may appear, these plants are tough, capable of withstanding drought and heat with little maintenance. Some plants, such as snow-on-the-mountain, have succulent leaves and stems that retain water, while others, such as the Mexican daisy, have wiry stems and thin, tough leaves that resist water loss. Plants such as calendula shade the soil with their dense foliage.

Both watering and fertilizing can be kept to a minimum in this garden. Removing spent blossoms will keep plants flowering continuously. Most of the plants featured here can be used for cut flowers. Statice, for example, makes a beautiful cut or dried flower. Experimenting with different annuals in successive years will give you a number of possibilities for filling your summer border. 🌸

SILVER CUP MALLOW
Lavatera trimestris **'Silver Cup'**
30-36 inches tall
All zones
Silvery pink, cup-shaped, 2-inch flowers along upright flower stalks all summer; rounded, dark green leaves on many-branched, hairy stems; poor to average, well-drained soil; full sun; low water. Water sparingly—prefers dry, hot conditions. Remove faded flower stalks.

CALENDULA (POT MARIGOLD)
Calendula officinalis
10-12 inches tall
All zones
Self sowing 2- to 4-inch flowers all summer in various colors, including pale and creamy yellows; deep green, oval leaves; poor to average, well-drained soil; full sun/light shade; low water. Remove faded blooms and pinch back terminal growth. Tangy, edible blossoms.

STATICE
Limonium sinuatum
30-36 inches tall
All zones
Tiny, lavender, papery flowers forming an attractive cluster all summer; coarse, deep green basal leaves with winged flower stalk; average, well-drained soil; full sun; minimal water. Flowers good for cutting and drying.

MEXICAN DAISY (MEXICAN FLEABANE)
Erigeron karvinskianus
12-18 inches tall
All zones
Daisy-like, ¾-inch, white flowers all summer turn pink then soft purple; hairy, narrow, oval leaves on mounding, airy plants; poor to average, well-drained soil; full sun; minimal water. All flower colors on plant at once. Performs best in hot, dry conditions. Self-sows. Perennial in Zones 8-10.

SNOW-ON-THE-MOUNTAIN (GHOST-WEED)
Euphorbia marginata
2 feet tall
All zones
Insignificant flowers; pointed, oval leaves with white edges, terminal clusters very distinctively white; poor to average, well-drained soil; full sun; low water. Water only when dry. Stems contain latex known as a skin irritant. Wear gloves when handling and use caution.

Showy Annual Edging

THIS GARDEN THRIVES WITH

SUN	WATER	SOIL
Part	**Medium to high**	**Average to rich**

In the spring, before your ornamental shrubs bloom, enjoy the showy presentation of an early flowering edging. Choose a location where trees will provide filtered shade during the hottest part of the day, since the plants featured here will not tolerate direct sun for more than 2 to 4 hours daily over a long period of time. Plants in this garden will perform best in cool, moist areas of the country. In warmer areas, you may want to substitute heat-tolerant summer annuals. If this is the case, plant your edging in full sun.

This brightly colored edging creates visual interest and separation between the green lawn and the green foliage of the shrub border. To avoid clashes, choose flowers that complement the border colors already in place. The red, yellow, and blue flowers here serve to refine the vibrant pinks of the azaleas and rhododendrons when they are in bloom.

You may want to vary the width of your edging, as shown here, so it won't look lost in front of larger plants with coarse foliage. This border is 2 feet wide near smaller-leaved azaleas but widens to over 3 feet in front of the rhododendrons. You can adjust your own edging width to suit your style and situation.

1. In the fall, using a hose and lime, mark serpentine shape 10 feet long, increasing from 2 feet wide at the start to 42 inches at its widest, then decreasing to 3 feet wide at the opposite end. Remove sod, till soil to 1 foot deep, cover with 4 to 6 inches of compost, and retill the top 6 inches of soil.

2. Beginning at back left, plant 6 daffodils (A) 6 to 10 inches deep, 4 to 6 inches apart and 4 inches from the back edge.

3. In spring, plant 1 blue and 1 pink forget-me-not (B) left of daffodils, spacing plants 8 inches apart. Along front edge, plant 3 rows of forget-me-nots 8 inches apart, alternating colors as follows: Row 1—Plant as follows: blue, pink, blue, pink, white. (You will extend this row in Step 4.) Row 2—Alternate 1 blue, 1 white to the end of the row. Row 3— Plant 1 blue, 1 white, and 1 blue forget-me-not.

4. Plant the remaining 13 blue forget-me-nots along the outside garden edge, as the continuation of Row 1.

5. Plant wallflowers (C) in rows 1 foot apart, as shown. Begin with yellow and alternate colors (4 yellow, 4 red). In a second row, begin with 2 yellow wallflowers, then alternate colors, ending with 2 yellow (6 yellow, 3 red). Finally, for the third row, plant 1 yellow and 3 red wallflowers above the last blue forget-me-not.

6. Mulch your garden with composted organic matter, bark nuggets, or other organic mulch and water well.

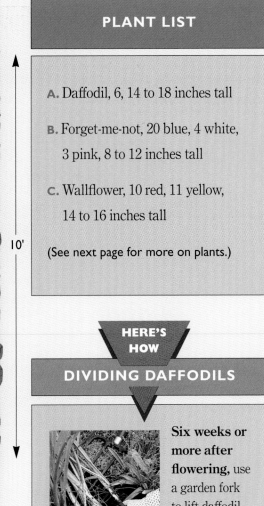

2' ← →

10'

← 3' →

PLANT LIST

A. Daffodil, 6, 14 to 18 inches tall

B. Forget-me-not, 20 blue, 4 white, 3 pink, 8 to 12 inches tall

C. Wallflower, 10 red, 11 yellow, 14 to 16 inches tall

(See next page for more on plants.)

HERE'S HOW

DIVIDING DAFFODILS

Six weeks or more after flowering, use a garden fork to lift daffodil bulbs after digging around clump 6 inches away from the foliage. Very gently, remove soil from bulbs, leaving roots attached. Split larger bulbs by pulling apart, gently untangling roots. Separate smaller bulbs if they come apart easily. Replant, spacing bulbs 4 to 6 inches apart, with pointed ends facing up.

Showy Annuals for Edging

Most of this showy edging can be planted as soon as the soil can be worked in the spring. The daffodils should be planted in the fall, as soon as the bed is made ready. All of these plants prefer cool daytime temperatures and moist soil. You will want to buy started plants from your local nursery, since wallflowers and forget-me-nots (biennials grown as annuals) must be started early in order to bloom the first year. In areas with cool summers, it is not necessary to replace these plants after they flower in the spring, although blooms will decrease.

Progression in texture, scale, and height are important elements of any garden's design. To maintain a balance, the taller wallflowers and daffodils are placed toward the rear of the border, against a background of large shrubs. Placed along the front of the garden, tiny-flowered forget-me-nots gracefully incorporate the edging into the larger border. ❧

DAFFODIL

Narcissus x incomparabilis **'Salome'**

14-18 inches tall

Zones 3-9

White flowers with apricot to pink trumpets edged with golden yellow on sturdy stems April to May; 4-inch-long, deep green, narrow, fleshy leaves; average to rich soil enriched with compost; full/part sun; medium water. Good cut flower. Remove seed heads but do not cut foliage back until completely yellow.

FORGET-ME-NOT

Myosotis sylvatica

8-12 inches tall

All zones

Pastel blue, pink, or white, fragrant flowers with yellow or white eyes May to June; dark green, lance-shaped leaves; average to rich soil enriched with compost; partial sun; medium water. Long-lasting cut flower. Likes cool, moist soil and conditions; self-sows in temperate, moist climates. Naturalizes in some areas.

WALLFLOWER

Cheiranthus cheiri

14-16 inches tall

All zones

Bright yellow or red, single, four-petaled, fragrant flowers April to May; 3 inch, deep green, narrow leaves; average to rich soil enriched with compost; full sun; medium water. Good cut flower. Dislikes dry soil and heat. Biennial treated as an annual. Self-sows.

CARE FOR YOUR SHOWY SPRING ANNUAL EDGING

SPRING Till under last winter's mulch or add organic matter to enrich soil. Mulch the garden again with 4 inches of compost, especially if it is in direct sun. In cool climates, plant when soil has warmed.

SUMMER Remove daffodil seed heads, trim foliage when completely yellow. Mark daffodils' location to avoid bulb injury. When annuals have finished blooming, remove and replace with summer-blooming plants.

FALL Remove dead plants, compost healthy debris after first frost. Mulch daffodils and bare soil with 4 inches of noncompacting compost for winter protection, soil nutrients, and to reduce topsoil loss. ❧

Alternative

SHOWY SUMMER ANNUAL EDGING

Even after the blooms of your wallflowers and forget-me-nots have faded, you can keep your edging bright with the easy substitutes shown here.

When you plant your summer edging, be sure to remove (by pinching or snipping) small flower buds or blossoms from newly purchased plants. This will increase their performance in the long run, making the plants healthier, bushier, and more productive. Also, if you plant your garden during hot weather, be sure to water the new plants thoroughly and frequently until they are well established. To help retain moisture, mulch the garden with several inches of compost.

These plants will provide summer flowers until frost. As an added attraction, all of the flowers can be cut for arrangements, and the cockscomb, which comes in either yellow or red, can be dried. Cutting flowers keeps the plants producing. Planting your edging a second time will allow you the full enjoyment of both the spring and summer seasons. 🐾

COCKSCOMB
Celosia cristata **'Yellow Castle'**
1-2 feet tall
All zones
Pyramid-shaped, feathery flower heads up to 6 inches in red, yellow, pink, or apricot summer to fall; oval, pointed, green leaves; average to rich, moist soil enriched with compost; full sun; low to medium water. Good cut or dried flower. Remove faded blossoms. Frost tender.

HELIOTROPE
Heliotropium arborescens **'Mini Marine'**
8-10 inches tall
All zones
Royal purple, fragrant flower clusters all summer; deep green, oval, heavily veined leaves on bushy plants; average to rich, moist soil enriched with compost; full sun; low to medium water. Long-lasting cut flower. Pot up for winter blooms. Deadhead blossoms for continuous flowering.

NASTURTIUM
Tropaeolum majus
1-2 feet tall
All zones
Upward-facing blooms all summer until frost with outward radiating petals, many colors from butter cream to scarlet; compact, deep green foliage; does well in poor soil; sun/light shade in hot areas; medium water. Flavorful and showy, edible flowers.

AGERATUM (FLOSSFLOWER)
Ageratum houstonianum
6-18 inches tall
All zones
Clusters of blue, lavender, or white, feathery, brush-like flower heads through summer into autumn; heart-shaped leaves; fertile, well-drained moist soil; full sun; medium water. Frost tender. Cut faded flowers for continuous blooms.

DALMATIAN BELLFLOWER
Campanula portenschlagiana
6-8 inches tall
Zones 5-7
Large clusters of erect, open, bell-shaped violet flowers late spring to summer; dense mat of ivy-shaped leaves; well-drained, gritty soil; partial shade; medium water. Vigorous, evergreen, prostrate perennial.

A Garden for Winter Interest

THIS GARDEN THRIVES WITH

SUN

Full

WATER

Low to medium

SOIL

Average to rich

Creating any garden is, in part, an exercise in architecture. A satisfying winter garden, without flowers to consider, depends even more on form, structure, layout, arrangement, and plant attributes. Paths, walks, gates, or other permanent features take on increased importance. Lighting, whether natural or artificial, will also change the look of your garden at different times of day. Elements of climate, such as fog, frost, mist, and snow, can outline, define, change, and enhance forms and shapes. Even garden fragrances change with cold temperatures and moist or dry air.

Locate your winter interest garden where it will be seen the most, whether you spend time indoors or out. If you will see your garden mostly from a distance, then larger, coarser plants are called for. In this garden, for example, large, mature evergreens create a background for the other plants. The ornamental grasses offer long-lasting, colored foliage and interesting shapes for months on end. Your winter planting will also attract wildlife, such as birds and small animals, for your enjoyment. You may even want to set out a bird feeder, winterized birdbath, or other encouragement for winter wildlife visitors.

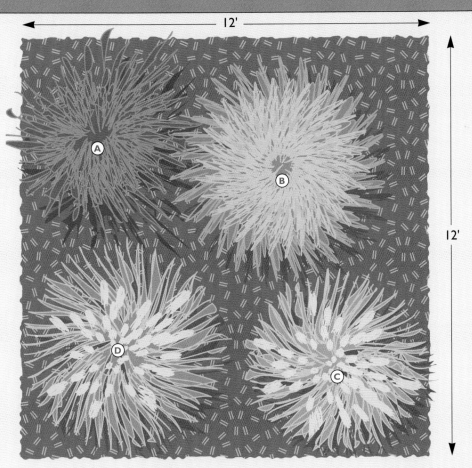

12'

12'

PLANT LIST

A. Hill's red cedar, 1, 6 to 12 feet tall

B. Dwarf blue spruce, 1, 10 to 15 feet tall

C. Maiden grass, 1, 4 to 5 feet tall

D. Pampas grass, 1, 5 to 6 feet tall

(See next page for more on plants.)

HERE'S HOW

CONTROL SPREADING GRASSES

Keep aggressive grasses from spreading by planting them in a 10- to 15-gallon plastic pot with the bottom removed. (Make sure pot does not have side holes for drainage.) Dig a hole the same size as pot. Place pot into hole, keeping the rim 1 to 2 inches above the soil. Backfill around pot edges, then fill it with a mix of garden soil and organic compost. Plant your ornamental grass in the center and water well.

1. In a sunny location with well-drained soil, as soon as soil can be worked, remove the sod from an area 12 x 12 feet. Till the soil 1 foot deep, add 4 inches of compost, and retill the soil to 4 inches deep.

2. Beginning at the back left-hand corner, plant a young Hill's red cedar (A) as deep as its rootball, 2 ½ feet from both the back and left side of garden. Stake (see Here's How, page 119).

3. Next, plant dwarf blue spruce (B) as deep as its rootball, 5 feet from both the back and right side of the garden. Stake as above.

4. Mulch the cedar and spruce with a 2- to 4-inch layer of shredded bark.

5. Plant the maiden grass (C) at the same depth it was planted in its container and 2 ½ feet from both the front and right sides of the garden.

6. Plant the pampas grass (D) at same depth it was planted in its container and 3 feet from both the front and left sides of the garden.

7. Mulch both grasses with 3 to 4 inches of organic mulch. Water entire garden thoroughly.

Plants for Winter Interest

Plants in your winter interest garden will provide you with beauty all year long. Evergreen conifers, such as the dwarf blue spruce and the red cedar used here, create a background for perennial grasses whose pale flowers would be lost in the winter landscape without background contrast. If your yard or garden doesn't have mature evergreens (they grow slowly), you may wish to choose faster growing dwarf varieties. Other good substitutes are such broad-leaved evergreens as rhododendrons or hollies, a dark wall, or perhaps a fence.

Ornamental grasses come in many different sizes. If the scale of your garden is not as large as the garden described here, consider using grasses with a smaller mature size, or adding perennials and smaller shrubs with winter interest in front of the grasses.

Grasses are virtually disease and pest free, and will tolerate drought. ❧

HILL'S RED CEDAR
Juniperus virginiana 'Hillii'
6-12 feet tall
Zones 2-9
Light blue, berry-like cones; prickly, blue-green needles, dense, columnar growth spreads with age; poor to average, well-drained soil; full sun; low to average water. Tolerates heat and drought.

DWARF BLUE SPRUCE
Picea pungens glauca 'Fat Albert'
10-15 feet tall
Zones 2-8
Dense, silvery blue needles on conical, squat tree; average to rich, well-drained, moist soil, but tolerates almost any soil; full sun; low to medium water. Most heat-tolerant spruce.

MAIDEN GRASS
Miscanthus sinensis 'Gracillimus'
4-5 feet tall
Zones 5-9
Long, white, fluffy flower heads July to August; narrow, arching leaves with distinct midrib, golden fall color; average, well-drained soil; full sun; low to average water. Tolerates heat and drought.

PAMPAS GRASS
Cortaderia selloana 'Pumila'
5-6 feet tall
Zones 6-10
Ivory white, ostrich-feather plumes 2 to 4 feet long, July to August; sharp-edged, arching leaves; average to rich, well-drained soil; full sun; low to average water. Tolerates heat and drought.

CARE FOR YOUR WINTER INTEREST GARDEN

SPRING Mulch grasses with compost or chopped leaves. Cut back last year's flowers and stalks. After the first winter, remove any stakes and wire supports from spruce and red cedar. Add woodchip mulch to suppress weeds.

SUMMER Water plants during hot, dry weather. Add compost or fertilizer if grass growth is weak or yellow. Remove invasive or aggressive spreading growth of grasses.

FALL Cut dried grasses for dramatic indoor arrangements. Leave remainder of seed heads and stems in your garden for structure and winter interest. Remove broken or bent flower stalks prior to onset of cold weather. ❧

Alternative

WINTER INTEREST PLANTS

You can choose the characteristics you would like your winter interest garden to have. If color is important to you, consider plants with long-lasting berries or fruits, colored foliage, or interesting bark. If shape and form intrigue you more, consider plants with unusual branch or stem structure. If you're a bird-lover, plants that provide protection, food, or nesting can be part of your plan. Sometimes one plant will satisfy a number of wishes, such as crab apple trees with both long-lasting fruits beloved by birds and attractively branched winter forms.

Shrubs and perennial plants can provide your winter garden with appealing dried leaves, flowers, and seed pods. Consider using hydrangeas or thistles for everlasting flowers, poppies or iris for seed pods, and small-leaved rhododendrons or hollies for colored leaves.

Winter light is different from summer light. The less direct sun casts longer shadows and shines through plants rather than on them, changing colors, contrasts, and forms. You may want to consider adding lighting to your yard and garden to brighten the long winter darkness. Combined with the reflective properties of snow, frost, and ice, upward lighting can illuminate an area and make your winter interest garden a spectacular sight day or night.

AMERICAN CRANBERRY BUSH
Viburnum trilobum
8-12 feet tall
Zones 2-8
White, 3- to 4-inch clusters of flat blossoms with showy outer flowers in May, followed by bright red, edible fruits; maple-like leaves with red tint, beautiful fall colors of yellow, red, and purple; average, moist, well-drained soil; part/full sun; medium water. Attracts birds.

AMUR CHOKECHERRY
Prunus maackii
35-40 feet tall
Zones 2-6
Small, white flowers in May followed by small, black cherries in August; deep green, oval leaves; well-drained, average soil; full sun; medium water. Shiny, coppery bark that peels and interesting, upright, branched form provide winter spectacle. Attractive to birds.

HONESTY (MONEY PLANT)
Lunaria annua
30-36 inches tall
Zones 4-9
Scented, white or purple four-petaled flowers in clusters May to June on stalks, followed by silvery, flat, oval seed pods; pointed, toothed, deep green leaves along stalks; average, well-drained soil; full sun/full shade but prefers partial shade; medium water. Self-sows prolifically.

BLUE OAT GRASS
Helictotrichon sempervirens
2 feet tall
Zones 4-10
Greenish, oat-like flowers on 4-foot, pale blue stalks only in colder climates during August; thin, spiky, blue, mound-forming leaves; fertile, well-drained soil; full sun; medium water. Withstands heat and drought.

Designing with Color

W hether you envision a riot of color or a soothing green oasis, designing a garden with color in mind is a challenge well worth the effort.

Successful color combinations among plants are based on the principles of harmony and contrast. When flowers of one hue are grown next to different flowers of a complementary hue the result is an intensely brilliant combination. And the closer plants are on the color wheel, the more harmonious the effect. Color may also be used as an enhancing accent.

Red is the most dominant of all garden colors and is often used as a single accent. A cascade of red climbing roses on a trellis, for instance, can attract the eye and dominate a view. But the same vivid color brushstroked through a cottage garden can enliven the entire planting. Most garden reds appear as shades or tints that can be effectively combined. Reds do well under sunlight but show up less in deep shade, where white impatiens make a bright accent.

You can give your garden exciting depths by taking advantage of special effects. For instance, if you place the gray-green foliage of dusty miller behind a bed of dark, low evergreens, your eye will be drawn past the evergreens to the light-colored dusty miller, creating the illusion of more depth in your garden. Foliage can also be a buffer between flower colors or can complement them. Although not as striking a design element as flowers, foliage is an essential element in your color scheme.

The designs in this section offer suggestions for contrasting as well as harmonizing the colors in your garden to create a balanced effect. Plan your own palette for striking seasonal or long-lasting color. ❧

A Cool Blue Flower Border

THIS GARDEN THRIVES WITH

SUN	WATER	SOIL
Part or full shade	Medium to high	Average to rich

In midsummer's heat, a border of flowers in refreshing shades of blue appears soothing and relaxing. Drifts of blue suggest tranquil shadows, calm water, and gentle shade.

This cool blue border needs a moist, partly shady area, but other blue borders can be grown in full sun or dry conditions. In moderate summer climates, a border like this one can tolerate more sun if large amounts of moisture are available. However, direct sunlight will affect the way in which blues and purples are seen, especially pastels or pale shades, which may look washed out or faded. In dappled sun or full shade, the same colors will appear more intense.

To choose harmonious hues for your blue border, avoid all brightly colored flowers. When small amounts of red or orange are used in a predominately blue garden, those colors will dominate, forcing blues into the background. Green and violet, both found along with blue on the cool side of the color wheel, create harmony because they both contain blue. Mixing dark and light hues of these colors will provide the variation you need for your cool border. In this garden, for example, color contrast is created by using lighter, purplish forget-me-nots and vivid, blue-violet bluebells. ❧

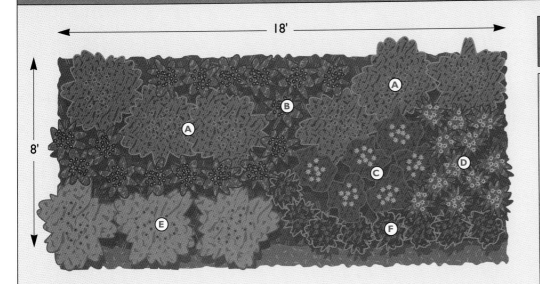

18'

8'

PLANT LIST

A. Blue hosta, 6, 3 feet tall

B. Royal blue forget-me-not, 16, 14 to 18 inches tall

C. Variegated hosta, 6, 2½ feet tall

D. Spanish bluebell, 12, 1½ feet tall

E. Gold hosta, 3, 2 feet tall

F. Bethlehem sage, 8, 1½ feet tall

(See next page for more on plants.)

HERE'S HOW

DIVIDING HOSTAS

1. In the spring, mark off an area 8 x 18 feet. Remove the sod, till soil, and then till in 3 to 4 inches of compost over the entire garden.

2. Plant 3 blue hostas (A) 3 feet apart starting in the back left corner and coming slightly forward, then 3 more starting from the back right corner.

3. Plant a staggered row of 2 forget-me-nots (B) along the middle of the left edge. Then plant 6 forget-me-nots along the back and 6 in front of the blue hostas on the left side, spaced 18 inches apart. Plant 2 more forget-me-nots between the groups of blue hostas.

4. Plant 1 variegated hosta (C) in front of the blue hostas on the right. In front of this one, offset 3 more variegated hostas 2 feet apart, then offset 2 more variegated hostas in front of the 3.

5. Plant 3 bluebells (D) on the right, in front of the blue hostas, then 3 staggered rows of 2 bluebells, and then 1 row of 3 in front of these.

6. Plant 3 gold hostas (E) along the left front of the garden.

7. Plant 6 Bethlehem sages (F) along the front on the right, and 2 more between the variegated and gold hostas.

8. Mulch entire garden and water plants thoroughly.

In early spring or late fall, dig up entire hosta crown. (In the fall, trim the leaves back to 2 to 3 inches.) Rinse the roots under running water to remove excess soil. Inspect the crown for natural divisions between the original plant and healthy new parts. Using a clean, sharp knife, separate the plant into pieces. Make sure shoots, crowns, and roots are all included in each new plant division. Reset pieces in the soil at the same depth as the parent plant.

Cool Blue Ideas

The perennial plants in this border will all increase in size each year. Many perennials, including hostas, can remain undisturbed for several years. However, dividing hostas rejuvenates them and provides you with new plants.

In this blue garden, foliage is as important as flowers. It can maintain the blue color theme and create interest even when nothing is in bloom. The blue-leaved hosta anchors that color in the border all season and provides texture with its large, veined, blue-green leaves. You may choose to replace the 'Gold Standard' here with another variety.

Select other perennials and self-seeding annuals in different shades of blue and in different sizes and shapes, such as bluebells and forget-me-nots. Include plants with unique foliage, such as the silver-spotted lungwort.

Some annuals in the blue color range, such as lobelias, salvias, or blue marguerites, will assist your perennials by blooming throughout the entire season. 🐾

BLUE HOSTA (BLUE PLANTAIN LILY)
Hosta sieboldiana
3 feet tall
Zones 3-9
White, bell-shaped flowers above foliage July; large, blue, veined leaves; average to rich, moist soil; part sun/full shade; medium water.

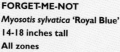

FORGET-ME-NOT
Myosotis sylvatica 'Royal Blue'
14-18 inches tall
All zones
Blue flowers April to June; lance-shaped leaves; average to rich, moist soil; part sun/shade. Long-lasting cut flowers. Self-sows and naturalizes.

VARIEGATED HOSTA (VARIEGATED PLANTAIN LILY)
Hosta 'Francee'
2 ½ feet tall
Zones 3-9
Lavender flowers on 3-foot stalks above foliage July to August; large, green leaves with white margins; average to rich, moist soil; part sun/full shade; medium water.

GOLD HOSTA (GOLD PLANTAIN LILY)
Hosta fortunei 'Gold Standard'
2 feet tall
Zones 3-9
Pale lavender flowers on 3-foot stalks August to September; average to rich, moist soil; part sun/part shade; medium water.

SPANISH BLUEBELL (WOOD HYACINTH)
Endymion hispanicus
1 ½ feet tall
Zones 5-9
Blue-violet flowers on slender stalks May to June; strap-shaped leaves; average to rich, moist soil; part sun/full shade; medium water. Naturalizes.

BETHLEHEM SAGE (LUNGWORT)
Pulmonaria saccharata 'Mrs. Moon'
1 ½ feet tall
Zones 4-8
Pink, 1-inch flowers May to June fade to blue; silver-spotted, green leaves; average to rich, moist soil; partial sun/full shade; medium water.

CARE FOR YOUR COOL BLUE BORDER

SPRING Remove protective winter mulch. Cultivate between plants to remove weeds, and place organic mulch around plants. Use compost as mulch since some of these plants are heavy feeders. Bark chips look attractive and can be used over the compost.

SUMMER Remove faded blossoms from Bethlehem sage, bluebells, and hostas before seeds form. Allow seeds to set on forget-me-nots except in cooler climates, where a second bloom is possible. Trim tattered leaves and check for slugs or snails on hostas. Water as necessary.

FALL Scatter the dried seeds from forget-me-nots over your garden before you mulch again. Remove any dead foliage and flower stalks. Cut perennials to within 4 inches of the ground. 🐾

Alternative

A COOL WHITE BORDER

Drifts of white flowers appear as cool as ocean foam on a hot summer day. Silver, gray, or bluish foliage mixed into a white perennial border creates a garden area that is both crisp and cool all season. The arching form of variegated sedge leaves suggests moving water in a fountain, while the tall, feathery flower spikes of goatsbeard lend an airy note to your summer border.

This border needs a moist location with full to partial sun. In bright sunlight, pure white flowers can seem to glow. They can also catch and reflect moonlight, garden, or streetlights, making a white border radiant at night. Sweet fragrances from the phlox and iris will scent the warm evening air.

You may also want to integrate white accents, such as trellises and pebble paths, into the garden at appropriate spots to complete the mood. ❧

SIBERIAN IRIS
Iris sibirica **'White Swirl'**
2-4 feet tall
Zones 3-9
White flowers with yellow markings on falls, June to July; narrow, grass-like, deep green foliage forming upright clumps; average to rich, moist soil; full sun/part shade; medium to high water. Tolerates wet conditions. Remove seed pods to increase plant vigor.

VARIEGATED SEDGE
Carex morrowii **'Variegata'**
12-18 inches tall
Zones 5-8
Insignificant flowers; narrow, arching, white leaves with green margins forming clumps; average to rich, moist or wet soil; full sun/part shade; medium to high water. Can tolerate standing water up to 4 inches deep.

GARDEN PHLOX
Phlox paniculata **'Mount Fuji'**
3-4 feet tall
Zones 2-8
Fragrant, pure white, terminal flower clusters June to September; lance-shaped, green leaves with distinct midrib; average to rich, moist soil; full sun/partl shade; medium water. Give plants adequate spacing to prevent mildew.

GOATSBEARD
Aruncus dioicus
4-6 feet tall
Zones 3-9
Large, white, feathery flower spikes 2 feet above foliage June to July; large, fernlike, deep green, compound leaves; average to rich, moist soil; part sun/part shade; medium to high water. In warmer climates, plant in shade and provide extra water.

ROSE MALLOW
Hibiscus moscheutos
3-4 feet tall
Zones 5-9
Large white flowers July to August with distinct white stamens and red eyes; large, oval green leaves on branched stems; average to rich, moist soil; full sun/part shade; medium to high water. Avoid windy locations where blossoms can be tattered. Plants increase in size with age.

ASTILBE
Astilbe x *arendsii* **'Bridal Veil'**
3-4 feet tall
Zones 4-8
White, fluffy, arching, feathery plumes above foliage July to August; dense, fernlike, deep green foliage sometimes tinged purple or red; average to rich, moist soil; part sun/full shade; medium to high water. Good cut or dried flower.

A Brilliant Blue and Gold Border

THIS GARDEN THRIVES WITH

SUN — Full or part

WATER — Medium

SOIL — Average, well drained

Color contrasts make blue and gold borders popular, and are a great way to brighten up a drab, green hedge. Blue and gold choices include blues and purples, as well as ivory, yellows, and oranges. These basic garden colors are available in varying intensities, from soft pastels to deep, intense hues. In this garden, blue-purple beard-tongue and reddish purple ornamental onion offer subtle variations in blue, and intensities vary from the soft yellow of dusty meadow rue to the deep purple catmint.

Tall plants, such as the violet-blue goat's-rue and the dusty meadow rue, dominate the back of the border. Side by side, their contrasting colors form the backdrop for the border, bringing both color and structure to this area. The hedge behind the border accentuates the flower colors by providing a continuous band of green foliage.

When planning your border, choose plants that span the blue and gold color ranges from pale pastels to deep, dominant hues. Avoid concentrating light or dark colors together in one spot. Instead, spread them throughout. You will find that this will keep your border visually balanced and pleasing. 🌸

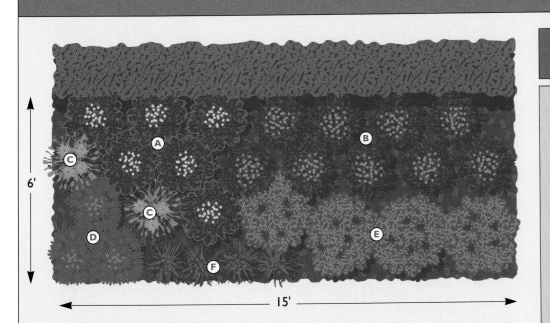

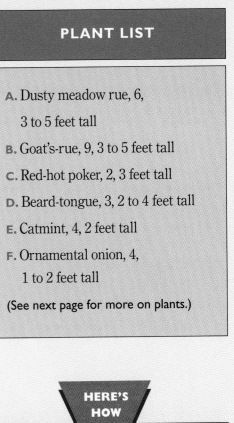

PLANT LIST

A. Dusty meadow rue, 6,
   3 to 5 feet tall

B. Goat's-rue, 9, 3 to 5 feet tall

C. Red-hot poker, 2, 3 feet tall

D. Beard-tongue, 3, 2 to 4 feet tall

E. Catmint, 4, 2 feet tall

F. Ornamental onion, 4,
   1 to 2 feet tall

(See next page for more on plants.)

1. In an area 6 x 15 feet, remove sod, till the soil, and add 3 inches of compost. Retill the soil, mixing in compost well.

2. In front of the hedge, starting on the left, plant a row of 3 dusty meadow rues (A) and 4 goat's-rues (B), spacing each plant 2 feet apart.

3. In front of this row, starting on the left, offset a row of 1 red-hot poker (C), 2 dusty meadow rues, and 5 goat's-rues. Space each plant 2 feet apart.

4. Offset a partial row in front of this row, starting on the left, by planting 1 beard-tongue (D), 1 red-hot poker, 1 dusty meadow rue, and 1 catmint (E) spaced 2 feet apart.

5. Offset the front row by planting from the left 2 beard-tongue, spaced 2 feet apart, and a line of 4 ornamental onions (F), spaced 1 ½ feet apart.

6. Continue the front row by planting on the right side 3 catmints, spacing plants 2 ½ feet apart.

7. Mulch the garden with a 3-inch layer of organic mulch such as wood chips or chopped leaves, and water well.

HERE'S HOW

CUT FLOWERS FOR ARRANGEMENTS

Any plant in this border will make a beautiful addition to a cut flower arrangement. Early in the morning or late in the evening, cut the flower stems 4 to 6 inches longer than the desired length for the arrangement. Cut the stems on an angle just prior to placing them in water and remove all lower leaves. Be sure to cut a variety of different shapes, such as rounded ornamental onions, spiky red-hot pokers, and feathery dusty meadow rues as fillers.

Striking Blue and Gold Flowers

Informal borders are achieved by careful planting of large areas, or masses, of color. Tall plants, such as dusty meadow rue and goat's-rue, dominate the back of the border with their contrasting colors, providing a backdrop for the other plants. Brightly colored flowers are separated by masses of flowers and foliage in subdued shades to minimize color clashes.

Stake the dusty meadow and goat's-rues early in the season so that the supports will be hidden beneath their foliage. Tall, sturdy plants, such as red-hot poker, provide additional support for the dusty meadow rue behind.

The plants in this border require little care other than to provide regular watering during dry periods and to remove faded flowers or undesired seed heads. Locate your border where it will receive dappled sun or afternoon shade if you live in a region with hot summers. ❧

DUSTY MEADOW RUE
Thalictrum speciosissimum
3-5 feet tall
Zones 5-9
Fluffy, yellow, fragrant flowers July to August; blue-green, glossy, fine foliage; average, well-drained, moist soil; full/part sun; medium water.

GOAT'S-RUE
Galega officinalis
3-5 feet tall
Zones 6-8
Violet blue, lilac, white, or bicolored pea-like flowers in spikes July to August; fine, divided, oval leaves; average, well-drained, moist soil; full/part sun; medium water. Remove seed pods.

RED-HOT POKER
Kniphofia uvaria **'Springtime'**
3 feet tall
Zones 5-9
Flowers are bright coral blending to yellow on spiky stems July to August; gray-green, grass-like clumps of foliage; average, well-drained, moist soil; full/part sun; medium water.

BEARD-TONGUE
Penstemon cobaea
2-4 feet tall
Zones 5-9
Blue-purple spikes of tubular flowers with a lighter lip July to August; glossy, lance-shaped leaves; average, well-drained, moist soil; full/part sun; medium water.

CATMINT
Nepeta x faassenii **'Dropmore'**
2 feet tall
Zones 5-9
Deep purple spikes of flowers July to August; gray-green, aromatic, oval leaves; average, well-drained, moist soil; full/part sun; medium water. Cut back faded flower spikes.

ORNAMENTAL ONION
Allium pulchellum
1-2 feet tall
Zones 6-9
Reddish purple, drooping flowers form a rounded head July to August; a rosette of narrow, dark green leaves; average, well-drained, moist soil; full/part sun; medium water.

CARE FOR YOUR BLUE AND GOLD BORDER

SPRING Remove winter mulch, then add 1 to 2 inches of compost and work into soil between plants. Remove unwanted volunteer seedlings and add organic mulch to border to help soil retain moisture. Stake rue plants when 1 to 2 feet tall.

SUMMER Water border regularly, especially when weather is hot and dry. Replenish mulch if necessary. Fertilize the garden twice prior to blooming with a liquid fertilizer that can be applied when you are watering.

FALL Cut back faded flowers and remove unwanted seed heads, especially from the invasive rues. Remove dead plants after first frost. Mulch garden for winter with a non-compacting mulch, such as straw, held in place with pine boughs. ❧

Alternative

A BRILLIANT PINK AND YELLOW BORDER

For another popular color combination, try these pink and yellow flowers. Less of a direct contrast than blue and gold, bright pinks and yellows can dominate a summer border, especially in bright sunlight. Yellows and pinks appear more vibrant in the summer than in the spring and fall.

Break up drifts of intense color with pastel blooms or foliage plants. The foliage of taller leafy plants such as golden thistle acts as a buffer when planted near brightly colored flowers. The silvery gray foliage of rose campion helps to cool down its vivid magenta blossoms. Lady's-mantle, a foliage plant with delicate sprays of yellow flowers, makes an excellent companion to many bright blooms.

Stark contrasts may be reduced by seasonal changes in blossom colors. The intense yellow of 'Moonshine' yarrow early in the season fades to a softer yellow as the season progresses. The color contrast between yarrows and nearby cranesbill will change as the yellow yarrow blooms fade and the red fall foliage of the cranesbill begins to emerge. 🌾

ROSE CAMPION
Lychnis coronaria
2 ½ feet tall
Zones 4-9
Magneta, 1-inch, circular flowers July to September; silvery, gray-green, soft leaves forming a rosette; average, well-drained, moist soil; full sun; medium water.

YARROW
Achillea x hybrida **'Moonshine'**
2 feet tall
Zones 4-9
Bright yellow, flat flower clusters on wiry stems July to August, fading to lemony yellow; gray-green, fernlike foliage; average, well-drained, moist soil; full/partial sun; medium water. Good dried flower.

CRANESBILL
Geranium sylvaticum
1 ½ feet tall
Zones 4-10
Deep pink, 1- to 2-inch, 5-petaled flowers July to August; dark green, toothed, divided leaves turning red in the fall; average, well-drained, moist soil; full/part sun; medium water.

LADY'S-MANTLE
Alchemilla mollis
1 ½ feet tall
Zones 4-9
Greenish yellow, tiny sprays of flowers up to 6 inches across June to August; rounded, green leaves with wavy margins forming dense mounds; average, well-drained, moist soil; full/part sun; medium water.

GOLDEN THISTLE
Centaurea macrocephala
4 feet tall
Zones 4-9
Bright yellow, 4-inch, thistle-like flowers on tall, strong stems July to August; 6- to 12-inch, coarse, dark green leaves with wavy margins; average, well-drained, moist soil; full/part sun; medium water. Good dried flower.

A Colorful Island

THIS GARDEN THRIVES WITH

SUN
Full

WATER
Medium

SOIL
Average to rich

An island bed, a garden surrounded by lawn or paving, can be a colorful or calm focal point in your home landscape. Islands can be as large or as small as you wish and in whatever shape that takes your fancy. But you may want to start with a small, easy-care island that you can enlarge over time.

Choose your location first, then select plants that suit your conditions. For example, for a fairly well-drained, sunny site, choose plants that tolerate heat well and need only moderate amounts of water. If your spot is shady and cool, look for shade-tolerant plants that like moisture, such as hostas and ferns.

Since island beds will be seen from many angles, you will generally want to locate taller plants near the bed's center and shorter plants around the outside. In the case of this colorful island, the tall cleome is used off-center but, since its stalks are slender and the plants are spaced apart, no view is obscured.

Consider a bed shape that can be mowed around easily, such as an oval or circle. Sharp corners may need to be hand-trimmed. Use of an edging will define your island bed and help prevent invasion by grass (see Here's How, page 67).

9'

PLANT LIST

A. Cleome, 3 white, 3 pink,
3 to 4 feet tall

B. Snapdragon, 12 mixed colors,
2 to 3 feet tall

C. Threadleaf coreopsis, 5,
2 feet tall

D. Ageratum, 11, 10 inches tall

E. Geranium, 12 electric red,
1 to 2 feet tall

(See next page for more on plants.)

1. Drive a stake into the center of the area in which you want your new garden bed and attach a 4 ½-foot string. Use lime to mark a circle on the ground as you walk around the 9-foot diameter.

2. Remove sod, working from the outside border toward the center. Till the soil, cover garden with 3 to 4 inches of compost, and till again.

3. Beginning at the right back of the circle, alternate planting 2 pink and 2 white cleomes (A) 18 inches apart, along the perimeter. Plant 1 white and 1 pink cleome to the left of the center 2 cleomes on the perimeter.

4. Along the left back perimeter and 1 foot apart, plant 6 snapdragons (B), a row of 4 in front of them, and then a row of 2, as shown.

5. Plant 2 coreopsis (C) 18 inches apart, in front of the 2 cleomes. Offset a row of 3 coreopsis in front and to the left of the first 2 coreopsis.

6. Plant 11 ageratums (D) 1 foot apart, along the front perimeter of your garden bed.

7. Plant a row of 9 geraniums (E) 1 foot apart and 1 foot behind the ageratum. Plant 2 more on the left in back of the geranium row and 1 more on the right in back of the geranium row, as shown in illustration.

8. Mulch the entire garden and water thoroughly.

HERE'S HOW

SIMPLE BRICK EDGING

For a permanent outline to your bed, try an attractive brick edging. Dig a trench 5 inches deep around the garden edge. Make it the width of two bricks laid side by side. Add 2 inches of sand to the bottom of the trench. Make a single row by positioning hard-fired, landscape bricks end to end on one side of the trench, each brick level with the soil surface. Make a second row around the edge, next to these. Backfill and tamp soil to secure the edging.

Plants for an Island Bed

This colorful island bed will bloom all summer with little care. The annual cleomes, geraniums, snapdragons, and ageratums will provide color from spring until frost if flowers are removed as they fade. Near the end of the season, allow a few cleomes and snapdragons to set seed for volunteer seedlings next spring.

In the island's center, perennial coreopsis blooms from June to frost. Coreopsis, like all perennials, can remain undisturbed for years. Because of its location, the remainder of this garden can be filled with annuals each spring without injuring the coreopsis. Should you choose to add other perennials to your island bed, cluster them together and mark their location in the fall to avoid digging them up by mistake in the spring before they have begun to grow.

With full sun and regular watering, this island garden will thrive.

CLEOME (SPIDER FLOWER)
Cleome hasslerana
3-4 feet tall
All zones
Slender, protruding stamens, bright pink or white petals on flowers June to frost; aromatic leaves, tall stems; poor to average, well-drained soil; full sun; low to medium water. Self-sows easily.

SNAPDRAGON
Antirrhinum majus '**Liberty Mixed**'
2-3 feet tall
All zones
Flowers like hinged lips, many colors, abundant blooms all summer on terminal spikes; lance-shaped, sticky foliage; average to rich, well-drained soil; full sun; medium water.

THREADLEAF COREOPSIS
Coreopsis verticillata '**Moonbeam**'
2 feet tall
Zones 4-10
Pale yellow, daisy-like flowers June to September; feathery, mounding, gray-green foliage; poor to average, well-drained soil; full sun; medium water. Divide every 2 to 3 years.

AGERATUM (FLOSSFLOWER)
Ageratum houstonianum
10 inches tall
All zones
Fluffy, blue flower clusters all summer; heart-shaped, hairy foliage; average to rich, well-drained soil; full sun; medium water.

GERANIUM
Pelargonium x hortorum '**Neon Rose**'
1-2 feet tall
All zones
Electric red flower clusters on strong stems all summer; rounded, lobed, green leaves may be reddish tinged; average, well-drained soil; full sun; medium water.

CARE FOR YOUR ISLAND BED

SPRING Remove the winter mulch. Till the soil around perennial coreopsis without disturbing its roots. Add a 2- to 4-inch layer of compost to the soil and retill. Mulch the entire garden after you have finished planting.

SUMMER Water garden thoroughly and regularly, especially during dry, hot weather. Add fertilizer and renew mulch as needed. Remove the faded flowers to promote continuous blooms.

FALL Remove dead plants and compost healthy plant debris. Use noncompacting mulch to cover coreopsis for the winter. In windy areas, cover exposed soil with mulch held in place with pine boughs.

Alternative

A FOLIAGE ISLAND

Use foliage plants to create an unusual garden island for your full-sun location. Foliage plants come in a wide range of colors, forms, and textures, making it easy to combine plants with different characteristics for contrast. For example, plant the upright, fine-textured annual kochia as a centerpiece in combination with a low, rounded, coarse-textured ornamental cabbage border. Add purple basil and blue rue along with the whitish, gray-green dusty miller for different textures and colors.

Most foliage plants have insignificant flowers. Some, such as ornamental cabbage and purple basil, must have their flower stalks removed or they will die. Pinch back terminal growth on upright plants when transplanting to encourage bushiness.

Foliage plants can be either annual or perennial. Some annual plants have an amazing tolerance for cold temperatures. Ornamental cabbage, for example, withstands frost and can be grown all winter in warm climates. Other plants change color in the fall. Kochia, for example, remains green all summer then turns brilliant red when autumn arrives. 🌾

PURPLE BASIL
Ocimum basilicum **'Purpurascens'**
2 feet tall
Zone 5
Insignificant flowers; dark purple, fragrant foliage on erect, branching stems; moderately rich, well-drained soil; full sun; medium water. Transplant this herb after soil is warm and pinch terminal growth. Remove flower stalks. Frost tender.

ORNAMENTAL CABBAGE (ORNAMENTAL KALE)
Brassica oleracea **'Northern Lights'**
12-18 inches tall
All zones
Insignificant flowers; large, brightly colored, crinkly leaves, fringed edges in combinations of green, red, pink, and white; average to rich, well-drained soil; full sun; medium water. Remove flower stalks. Tolerates cold temperatures.

RUE
Ruta graveolens **'Jackman's Blue'**
1 ½-2 feet tall
Zone 5
No flowers; blue, fernlike, strong-scented foliage on compact and bushy plants; average, well-drained soil; full/part sun; medium water. Protect in cold winter zones. Skin contact may cause rash, so wear gloves and use care when handling.

KOCHIA (RED SUMMER CYPRESS)
Kochia scoparia form *trichophylla*
3 feet tall
All zones
Insignificant flowers; narrow, oval, light green leaves turn brilliant red in the fall; average to rich, well-drained soil; full/part sun; medium water. Also known as 'Burning Bush' but is not the perennial. Self-sows easily.

DUSTY MILLER
Senecio cineraria **'Silverdust'**
1 foot tall
All zones
Insignificant flowers; grown for its velvety, stiff, finely cut, silvery white foliage; average to rich, well-drained soil; full sun/part shade; medium water. Pinch back when transplanting to achieve short, bushy plants.

A Multicolored Border

THIS GARDEN THRIVES WITH

SUN
Full

WATER
Low to medium

SOIL
Average, well drained

As the spring soil begins to warm, consider planting a multicolored border to provide nonstop color until frost. Locate your garden in front of a wall, fence, line of shrubs, or a tall perennial bed as a backdrop. Choose an open, sunny site where the border will receive at least 6 hours of direct sunlight during the growing season.

In this garden, colors were chosen to complement background perennials. Select only three or four colors and allow natural variations to fill in the palette. Red, for example, can include orange, scarlet, ruby, burgundy, pink, and purple. Flowers come in such an infinite range of tints and shades that almost any two colors can be combined felicitously. Weave each color throughout the bed to create pattern and visual flow, and consider whites and gray-blues as harmonizers. In this garden, white petunias and blue salvia act as counterpoint to the reds.

Sometimes even small changes in a border, whether of color or form, can produce a more satisfying combination. Placing rounded petunias and globe amaranth flowers near spiky salvia exaggerates both plant and flower forms, adding interest and contrast to your border. Your backdrop will serve to frame and unify as you experiment. ❧

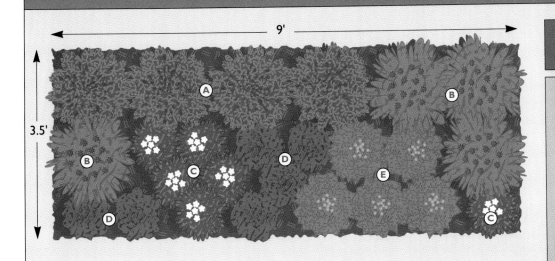

9'

3.5'

PLANT LIST

A. Salvia, 4 blue, 2 feet tall

B. Globe amaranth, 4 red, 2 feet tall

C. Petunia, 6 white, 14 inches tall

D. China pink, 6 red, 8 inches tall

E. Potentilla, 5, 1 foot tall

(See next page for more on plants.)

1. Mark an area 9 x 3 ½ feet. Remove sod, till soil, add 2 to 3 inches of compost, and retill the soil.

2. Begin at the back left side of garden: plant 4 salvias (A) in a row, spacing them 18 inches apart.

3. Plant 2 globe amaranths (B) 18 inches apart to the right of the salvias. Plant 1 globe amaranth on each side of the border.

4. Plant a row of 2 petunias (C), 1 foot apart, to the right of the leftmost single globe amaranth. Offset 2 and then 1 more petunia in front of these. Plant the last petunia in front of the globe amaranth on the right.

5. Plant 2 China pinks (D) 1 foot apart, starting at the left front row. Then plant 2 more pinks in the center, in front of the salvias and to the right of the petunias. Offset 1 pink in front of these, then plant 1 more offset pink in the front row.

6. Plant 3 potentillas (E) 18 inches apart in the front row. Then offset 2 more directly behind.

7. Mulch the garden with 2 to 3 inches of an organic mulch such as bark chips or compost; water thoroughly.

HERE'S HOW

SIMPLE METHODS TO STAKE PLANTS

Provide discrete staking for taller plants before they reach half their mature height. To create a simple structure, encircle the base of the plant with 1-inch-thick wooden or metal stakes up to approximately ¾ of the plant's mature height. Tie a series of strings connecting each stake every 3 to 6 inches of the stake's length. As the plant fills in, the support will become less noticeable.

Sensational Multicolored Bloomers

These plants will bloom continuously all season with a minimum of care. Although most of these plants can tolerate drought conditions, they will benefit from regular watering and an organic mulch. Plant them in well-drained soil and full sun, water regularly, and snip faded blossoms. Removing decaying or dead foliage and blossoms will lessen chances of disease or insect infestation and add to the attractiveness of your multicolored border.

To encourage vigorous plant and root growth, remove flower buds from newly purchased plants. New plants will establish themselves faster and produce more flowers over the growing season. Stake tall plants, such as salvias and globe amaranths (see Here's How, page 71).

The perennial salvia here, placed at the back of the garden, is protected when the annual area is cultivated the following spring. ❧

SALVIA (MEADOW SAGE)
Salvia x *superba* '**May Night**'
2 feet tall
Zones 4-9
Purplish blue, spiky flower stalks May to October; lance-shaped leaves; poor to average, well-drained soil; full sun; low to medium water. Tolerates heat and drought. Remove faded flowers.

GLOBE AMARANTH
Gomphrena globosa '**Strawberry Fields**'
2 feet tall
All zones
Red, 2- to 3-inch, round flowers on wiry stems all summer; oval leaves; poor to average, well-drained soil; full sun; low to medium water. Tolerates heat and drought. Good cut or dried flower. Remove faded blossoms.

PETUNIA
Petunia x *hybrida* '**Fantasy Ivory**'
14 inches tall
All zones
Many pure white, trumpet-shaped, 3- to 5-inch flowers all summer; sticky, hairy, deep green, oval leaves; average, well-drained soil; full sun; medium water. Cut back leggy growth for repeated flowering.

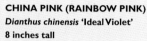

CHINA PINK (RAINBOW PINK)
Dianthus chinensis '**Ideal Violet**'
8 inches tall
All zones
Fragrant, 1-inch, single, red-violet flowers with fringed petals all summer; gray-green, narrow leaves; average, well-drained soil; full sun; low to medium water. Prefers alkaline soils.

POTENTILLA
Potentilla fruticosa '**Pyrenaica**'
1 foot tall
Zones 3-8
Golden yellow flowers all season; gray-green, lobed foliage; well-drained, rich, moist, slightly alkaline soil; full sun; medium water. Dwarf.

CARE FOR YOUR MULTICOLORED GARDEN

SPRING On established plants, pinch back terminal growth to keep plants bushy. Cultivate and add mulch. Remove flower buds on newly purchased plants. Add nutrients by incorporating compost or fertilizer into the soil.

SUMMER As the taller plants grow, be sure they are supported inside their stakes. Water plants regularly. Mulch with additional organic matter to supply necessary nutrients, retain moisture, and keep the soil cool.

FALL Remove dead plants after the first frost to discourage diseases and pests the following year. Compost healthy plants; bury others away from the garden. Mark location of perennials and mulch for winter protection. ❧

Alternative

A MULTIFACETED BORDER

Choosing plants that are useful as well as ornamental will make your multifaceted border serve more than one purpose. Fragrant or aromatic herbs with colorful flowers and leaves not only look beautiful but are also useful for herbal teas and culinary purposes. They can also deter insects and garden pests. Vegetables such as peppers and eggplants, if planted near herbs, will benefit from their insect-repelling properties and can be harvested over the growing season. Marigolds planted near tomatoes and purple basil will not only look spectacular but will help deter insects and disease.

Try fast-growing, early maturing vegetables along with herbs and flowers. Companion plants (lettuce and radishes, for instance) can be tucked into the garden space between other plants and make a living, edible mulch. Add flowering plants, such as hollyhocks, for height and old-fashioned charm.

Flowering herbs will bring birds and other wildlife to your garden. Red bee balm, for example, will attract hummingbirds. Strawberries, nasturtiums, and coriander are appealing to butterflies. Honeybees especially love borage. 🌿

BORAGE
Borago officinalis
2-3 feet tall
All zones
Star-shaped, 1-inch, blue flowers fading to pink; May to October; 4- to 5-inch, large, hairy, oblong leaves; average to rich, well-drained soil; full sun; medium water. Use fresh or cooked leaves as a vegetable and blossoms as garnish or in salads.

NASTURTIUM
Tropaeoleum majus
1 foot tall
All zones
Spurred, tubular, fragrant 2-inch blossoms of yellow, orange, red, pink, or cream May to October; 3- to 4-inch, round, green leaves; poor to average, well-drained soil; full sun; medium water. Tolerates dry conditions. Use leaves and flowers fresh in salads and for garnishes.

CORIANDER (CHINESE PARSLEY/CILANTRO)
Coriandrum sativum
2-3 feet tall
All zones
Tiny, white flowers in clusters May to August; glossy, green, lacy leaves; average to rich, well-drained soil; full sun; medium water. Seeds used for confections and in making curry. Leaves used in oriental and southwestern dishes.

BEE BALM (OSWEGO TEA)
Monarda didyma
2-4 feet tall
Zones 4-9
Red, pink, purple, or white, spiky-petaled, round flower clusters June to August; dark green, oval, pointed leaves; average to rich, well-drained soil; full sun; medium water. Dry flowers and leaves for tea; use leaves fresh in salads. Especially loved by hummingbirds.

EVERBEARING STRAWBERRIES
Fragaria x ananassa
6-8 inches tall
Zones 4-9
White, 5-petaled flowers with yellow centers May to September, followed by deep red, 2- to 3-inch, edible fruits June to October; three-lobed, shiny, dark green, rounded leaves; average to rich, well-drained soil; full sun; medium water. Spreads by runners.

A Complementary Color Border

THIS GARDEN THRIVES WITH

SUN	WATER	SOIL
Full	Medium	Poor to average

To brighten a monochromatic row of conifers, consider planting this complementary color border in front of it. Set against the soft, fine foliage of coniferous trees and shrubs, the border shown here combines two complementary colors to create a strong, eye-catching contrast.

Complementary color gardens contain combinations of colors that are opposite each other on the color wheel (see Here's How, page 75). Understanding color relationships will allow you to create inviting combinations in your garden plan. In this garden, fernleaf gold yarrow and daisy-like coreopsis are highlighted by the deep blue-purple spikes of salvia.

Use complementary color schemes in your garden to create a vibrant, intense design. True flower colors that are not pastels or mixes, such as bright yellow marigolds and dark purple salvias, create the strongest visual contrast. Use paler colors, such as lavender and creamy yellow, for a more subdued contrast. Before deciding upon your color combinations, think about the effect you want to create—subtle, bold, or something in between. With a little planning, color can add a punch to your garden and surrounding landscape. ❦

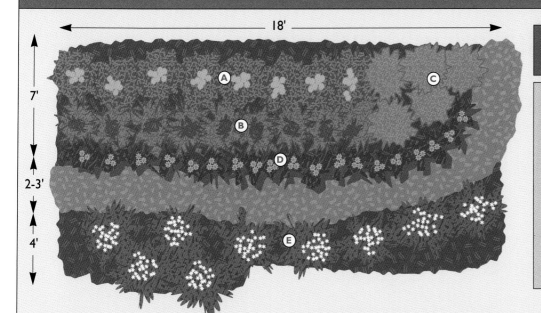

18'

7'

2-3'

4'

PLANT LIST

A. Fernleaf yarrow, 8, 3 feet tall

B. Salvia, 9, 2 feet tall

C. Artemisia, 5, 24 to 30 inches tall

D. Coreopsis, 19, 18 to 24 inches tall

E. Bumald spirea, 9, 2 to 3 feet tall

(See next page for more on plants.)

HERE'S HOW

USING THE COLOR WHEEL

1. Remove sod from an area 7 x 18 feet in front of background plants, taking care to stay beyond their dripline to avoid root injury. Till the soil, add 4 inches of compost, and retill the soil 4 to 6 inches deep.

2. Beginning 1 foot from the back left side, plant 8 yarrows (A) in a row, spacing them 2 feet apart.

3. Plant 9 salvias (B) in a row 18 inches apart, 3 feet in front of yarrows.

4. To the right of the row of yarrows plant 3 artemisias (C) spaced 18 inches apart. Plant 2 artemisias staggered in front of this row, as shown.

5. Next, plant a row of 19 coreopsis (D) 1 foot apart, ending in front of the artemisias as shown on diagram.

6. If you don't have a ready-made garden path, remove a strip of sod 2 to 3 feet wide in front of this planting

bed, as shown. Cover with 4 inches of fine gravel, level with a rake, and compact with a roller, if possible.

7. On the other side of the path, remove sod to create an area 3 x 18 feet. Enlarge the first 8 feet of the left side by an additional 1 foot. Till the soil, add 4 inches of compost, and retill the soil 4 to 6 inches deep.

8. Plant 7 spireas (E) 3 feet apart, as shown. Plant the 2 remaining spireas in the enlarged left edge of bed, staggering them in front of the first 3 spireas on the left.

9. Mulch plantings with compost. Water well.

The color wheel represents the spectrum of color that appears naturally in rainbows. The primary colors, red, blue, and yellow, are the starting points for every other color. To find a color's opposite or complementary color, draw a line from one color through the center of the wheel to the color directly opposite on the wheel.

Colorful Complementary Flowers

The perennials in this garden need full sun. Place them to the south of the conifers so sunlight is not blocked. Water your garden in dry weather and keep mulch at its original depth of 4 inches during the growing season to control weeds and conserve water.

Your complementary color border can also benefit by including harmonious colors. Placing yellow yarrow flowers in front of the green conifer needles, for instance, helps to keep this garden from becoming too flashy. Other foliage also helps to create harmony and tone down contrasts. The silvery artemisia and the blue-green leaves of the spirea are a restful counterpoint to more intense colors. Textures, such as conifer needles and the fine leaves of fernleaf yarrow and coreopsis, unify as well as please. Your complementary color border will be a bold yet subtle mixture that will delight the eye. 🌼

FERNLEAF YARROW
Achillea filipendulina **'Coronation Gold'**
3 feet tall
Zones 4-8
Golden, flat-headed flowers July to August; aromatic, fine leaves; poor to average, well-drained soil; full sun; medium water. Flowers dry well.

SALVIA (MEADOW SAGE)
Salvia x *superba* **'Blue Queen'**
2 feet tall
Zones 4-9
Spiky, deep blue-purple flowers above foliage June to September; thick, wrinkled basal leaves; ordinary soil; full/part sun; low to medium water. Drought resistant. Remove spent flower spikes.

ARTEMISIA (BEACH WORMWOOD)
Artemisia stellerana
24-30 inches tall
Zones 3-8
Tiny yellow, rounded flowers June to August; silvery gray leaves; poor to average, well-drained soil; full sun; medium water.

COREOPSIS (TICKSEED)
Coreopsis lanceolata
18-24 inches tall
Zones 4-9
Yellow, daisy-like flowers June to September; lance-shaped leaves; poor to average, well-drained soil; full sun; low to medium water.

BUMALD SPIREA
Spiraea x *bumalda*
2-3 feet tall
Zones 3-8
Flat terminal clusters, 4 to 6 inches long, of tiny white or pink flowers June to August; blue-green leaves, bronzy fall color; ordinary, well-drained soil; full/part sun; low to medium water.

CARE FOR YOUR COMPLEMENTARY COLOR BORDER

SPRING Remove the winter mulch and branches covering plants and use new mulch around the plants during the growing season. Pinch terminal shoots at second bud for bushier plants. Stake salvias and yarrows for upright growth.

SUMMER Water garden during hot, dry weather. Remove spent flowers for continuous blooms. Trim the plants occasionally during the growing season, to help keep them bushy, and prune spirea after flowering.

FALL Remove and dispose of diseased plant debris away from garden. Do not compost. Cut perennials within 3 to 6 inches from the ground. Use clean plant materials and conifer needles for mulch. Cover with conifer branches for extra winter protection. 🌼

Alternative

HARMONIOUS HUES

Harmonious, or analogous, hues are colors that appear side by side on the color wheel, such as red and purple or red and orange. Use harmonious hues to tame a high-contrast border that has too many bright flowers or to create an entire border with a soothing color theme. Think of the gentle transition of colors in a rainbow, where one color seems to blend seamlessly into the next.

Harmonious hues need not be pale or pastel, but they should be closely related, such as a progression of varying shades of blue to purple. The intense interaction found between complementary colors, such as blue and orange, is avoided in a composition using harmonious hues. The rule to follow for creating a harmonious hue garden is to avoid mixing colors that fall to both sides of the primary color. For example, in this garden the flower colors tend toward lavender, rose, and magenta, with nothing from the orange range.

All the plants suggested for this harmonious hue garden need a sunny location, average, well-drained soil, and regular watering if the weather is hot and dry. They will provide you with beautiful flowers in your garden throughout the growing season, cut flowers for indoor arrangements, and dried flowers for the fall and winter. 🌸

GAYFEATHER
Liatris spicata **'Kobold'**
2 feet tall
Zones 3-10
Upright, feathery, pinkish purple flowers July to frost; narrow leaves along stems; average, well-drained soil; full sun; medium water. Flowers attract butterflies and can be used for arrangements.

SEDUM
Sedum telephium **'Autumn Joy'**
18-24 inches tall
Zones 3-9
Large, pink flower clusters turning a deep reddish pink as they mature July to frost; succulent, silvery green foliage and leaves; average, well-drained soil; full sun; medium water. Flowers can be dried.

CORAL BELLS (Alumroot)
Heuchera **x** *brizoides* **'Snowstorm'**
15 inches tall
Zones 3-10
Small, bell-shaped, red flowers hanging from upright stalks June to September; white leaves with green margins and speckles; average to rich, well-drained soil; full sun/partial shade; medium water. Flowers can be cut and used for arrangements.

WEIGELA
Weigela florida **'Rubridor'**
3-4 feet tall
Zones 4-8
Many, tubular, 1-inch, reddish pink flowers May to June, sometimes repeats; oval, deep green leaves turn reddish purple in fall; tolerates less than ideal conditions but prefers average, well-drained soil; full sun/partial shade; medium water. Trim damaged twigs in spring.

MULLEIN PINK (Rose Campion)
Lychnis coronaria
2½ feet tall
Zones 4-9
Magenta flowers July to September on many-branched, woolly stalks rising from white, velvety leaves forming a clump; average, well-drained, moist soil; full sun; medium water. Self-sows.

Cascades of Color

An informal mix of flowers and foliage cascading from trellises and across your garden can accent a back door or shed, as they do here. Along with blooming vines, this planting features showy annuals for all-season color. The mixture of plants invites the use of many different hues simultaneously, including red, pink, yellow, purple, and orange. Bold green foliage and mounding plant forms also help this scheme succeed.

Repetition of its various colors keeps this planting cohesive. The red of the climbing rose is reflected in the petunias and echoed again in the nasturtiums and pansies. The purple clematis can be trained upright and then allowed to spill downward in a waterfall effect.

This plant assortment also provides textural contrasts. Coarse and fine foliage and flowers appear throughout the garden. Delicate pansy leaves and flowers, appropriately located along the front of the garden, are offset by the larger blooms of roses and clematis in the background.

Your cascading garden doesn't have to be planted from scratch. Start with just one or two cascading plants tucked into your permanent bed and add to your design each season. ❦

THIS GARDEN THRIVES WITH

SUN	WATER	SOIL
Full	Medium	Average, well drained

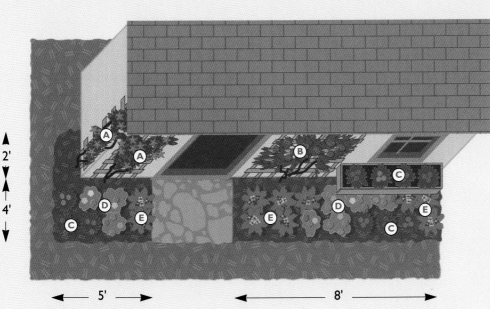

PLANT LIST

A. Clematis, 2, 10 feet tall

B. Climbing rose, 1, 10 feet tall

C. Petunias, 14 mixed
   colors, 10 inches tall

D. Nasturtium, 8 mixed colors,
   1 foot tall

E. Pansy, 10 mixed colors,
   6 to 12 inches tall

(See next page for more on plants.)

1. In an area 4 x 5 feet on one side of your back door and another area 4 x 8 feet on the other side, remove sod. On left side of house, remove sod from 2- x 1-foot area connected to front bed. In all areas, till the soil, add 3 to 4 inches of compost, and retill the soil.

2. Install trellises on either side of the door and around the left corner. Install window box.

3. Plant clematis (A) 6 inches away from the front of left trellises.

4. Plant the climbing rose (B) 12 to 18 inches away from the front of trellis on the right side of the door.

5. Plant 4 petunias (C) in the window box on the right and 4 more petunias (not shown) directly under the window box, starting on the right side of the climbing rose and running along by

the house to the right side of the large bed.

6. Plant the middle rows of both beds, spacing all plants 1 foot apart. Begin with 1 petunia, 2 nasturtiums (D), and 1 pansy (E). For the 8-foot middle row, begin on the bed's left and plant 3 pansies, 3 nasturtiums, then 2 pansies.

7. Plant the front rows of the garden with 2 petunias, 1 nasturtium, and 1 pansy. Then, in the bed on the right, plant 2 pansies, 2 nasturtiums, 3 petunias, and 1 pansy.

8. Mulch the entire garden. Water well until plants are established.

HERE'S HOW

CANDIED FLOWERS

For ornamental, edible candied flowers, cut pansy, violet, or nasturtium blossoms just after they have opened, leaving a ½-inch stem. Use flowers that haven't been sprayed with insecticide. Beat an egg white until fluffy and paint the blossoms with it, using a soft, clean paintbrush. Sprinkle the blossoms with extra-fine granulated sugar and allow to dry for 48 to 72 hours. Store in an airtight container. (Do not try with other flowers unless you are sure they are edible.)

Plants for Cascading Color

Blooms cascading from a trellis add charm to a variety of garden settings. In this planting, showers of roses and clematis are enhanced by beds of brightly colored annuals—petunias, nasturtiums, and pansies. All of these plants are popular and reliable performers, and you will find that caring for them is quick and easy.

Climbing roses and clematis provide vertical color in the garden, as will the window box full of cascading petunias. The flowering annuals in the beds not only create color but also provide necessary shade for the roots of the clematis. They also hide the bare lower stems of the climbing rose.

'Dortmund' roses are unusual in that they do not require full sun all day to perform reliably. This climber will provide a bounty of colorful, perfumed blooms throughout the summer. ❧

CLEMATIS
Clematis x jackmanii
10 feet tall
Zones 4-9
Purple, star-shaped, 6-inch flowers July to September; dark green, compound leaves; average, moist, well-drained soil; full sun/roots shaded; medium water. Provide a sturdy support.

CLIMBING ROSE
Rosa 'Dortmund'
10 feet tall
Zones 5-9
Single, red, 4-inch flowers June to August; glossy, green foliage; average to rich, moist, well-drained soil; full sun/partial shade; medium water. Remove spent flowers for longer blooming period.

PETUNIA
Petunia x hybrida 'Cascade Mix'
10 inches tall
All zones
Multicolored, trumpet-shaped, 3- to 5-inch flowers all summer; sticky, hairy, green foliage; average, well-drained soil; full sun; medium water. Cut back for repeat flowering.

NASTURTIUM
Tropaeoleum majus 'Alaska'
1 foot tall
All zones
Fragrant yellow, orange, red, pink, or cream spurred flowers all summer; unusual, rounded, green, edible foliage; poor to average, well-drained soil; full sun; low to medium water.

PANSY
Viola x wittrockiana 'Crystal Bowl'
6-12 inches tall
All zones
Brightly colored flowers all summer in cool climates, February to May in warm; lobed, green leaves form mounds; average to rich, well-drained soil; full sun/partial shade; medium water.

CARE FOR YOUR CASCADING GARDEN

SPRING Incorporate 1 to 2 inches of compost into the soil around clematis and rose plants, using care near roots. Remove dead canes on rose. Prune any dead stems on clematis. Mulch garden to conserve moisture and reduce weeds.

SUMMER Water garden regularly, especially during hot, dry weather, and fertilize. Remove spent blossoms and trim leggy growth from plants. Cut annuals back severely during warm weather to encourage strong regrowth and new blooms.

FALL Remove dead plants and compost if healthy. Dispose of rest away from the garden. Mound earth around the base of the rose canes for winter protection. After the clematis has died back, cover its roots with a mulch that won't compact. ❧

Alternative

AN EVERGREEN CASCADING GARDEN

Consider using evergreen shrubs and perennials to create cascading effects that will enhance your garden from season to season.

Some plants, such as pieris, are appealing even when they are not in flower. Cascades of light pieris buds against evergreen leaves are especially attractive during the winter, and a bonus occurs in the spring when new growth is distinctly red before it changes to dark green. Other plants, like 'Gold Coast', junipers with their weeping form, have colorful year-round foliage that becomes more pronounced during cold weather. The green leaves of wintercreeper vine grow purplish in the winter, and bergenia's deep green foliage in warm weather turns purplish-bronze as freezing occurs. Early in the spring, pink, red, or white bergenia flowers are striking against this foliage. While not a cascading plant, bergenia makes an excellent edging or ground cover, and it provides a nice contrast to the cascading form.

Fountain grass, with its overflowing effect, also is attractive all year. Its pinkish flowers fade as its foliage turns apricot in the fall. Atop wiry stems, the flowers are especially charming as they flutter in the winter wind. 🍃

CHINESE JUNIPER
Juniperus chinensis **'Gold Coast'**
3-5 feet tall
Zones 3-9
Insignificant flowers; yellow-tipped, dense needles on arching stems; poor to average, well-drained soil; full sun; medium water. Adapts to most situations.

FOUNTAIN GRASS
Pennisetum alopecuroides **'Morning Light'**
3 feet tall
Zones 5-10
Soft, pinkish buff, feathery flower spikes August to October above dark green foliage, with narrow, arching leaves in clumps forming a fountain shape; average, well-drained soil; full sun; low to medium water. Long-lasting winter plumes.

LEATHERLEAF BERGENIA
Bergenia cordifolia
1 ½ feet tall
Zones 4-8
Deep pink, red, purple, or white bell-shaped, 1 ½-inch flowers in clusters February to April; glossy, round, deep green foliage turns purple or bronze in winter; average to rich, moist soil; partial shade; medium to high water.

WINTERCREEPER
Euonymus fortunei
3-15 feet tall
Zones 4-9
Insignificant yellowish white blossoms June to July; 1- to 2-inch, dense, oval, dark green or variegated leaves; average, well-drained soil; full sun/part shade; medium water. A popular, evergreen shrub that can also be grown as a climber.

JAPANESE PIERIS (ANDROMEDA)
Pieris japonica
9 feet tall
Zones 4-8
White, cascading, fragrant flower clusters 3 to 6 inches long, March to April; foliage bronze or red when new, changing to glossy, dark green; fertile, well-drained, acidic soil; partial sun/partial shade; medium water. Prune after flowering.

Designing Around Features

Spectacular gardens are often created around unique garden elements such as water features, lighting, or specimen plants. To find a central focus for your garden, begin by assessing your walkways, entries, trees, mailboxes, lampposts, fences, and even rocks.

You can create a garden or landscape picture, for example, by using the principle of framing. Isolate an element in your garden—perhaps a venerable old tree—and give it star status. Special treatment might include encircling the tree with planting beds or benches, helping to make it a focal point in your garden. Contrast, another important design element, can be used to great effect as well. Lead the eye with a light-colored walkway in a shady area, for example, or enhance the light color of your front door with a planting of dark foliage.

Even problem areas can be transformed by clever treatment of special features. If you have too prominent a view of a neighbor's fence, emphasize a feature in your own landscape to direct attention where you want it. Or turn a rocky slope into an artful rock garden. Whatever your situation, use the ideas and projects in this section to create garden designs around your own property's unique features. ❦

A Textured Walkway

THIS GARDEN THRIVES WITH

SUN
Part sun to shade

WATER
Medium to high

SOIL
Average to rich

From the glossy, leathery foliage of Siberian bergenia to the silver-spotted leaves of Bethlehem sage, planning a textured walkway, such as the one shown here, will introduce you to another dimension of gardening. You can use the forms and colors of your plants and walkway materials as well as the light in an area to create a palette of exciting visual and tactile texture.

Vary leaf shape and surface quality, plant form, and flowers to provide a variety of sensations. Juxtapose large, coarse foliage against light and airy leaves to show each off to its best advantage. In this garden, the rounded, horizontal bergenia leaves contrast well with arching daylily clumps and spiky, upright ligularias.

By planting the edges of your path with plants whose colors contrast with the walking surface, you will add visual impact to both path and garden. For example, plant light-colored foliage or flowering plants next to dark surfaces and use light walkway surfaces for dark, shaded areas.

Low-growing plants work best placed immediately next to a walk. They help to define the walkway and provide a smooth transition from the surface of the path to taller plants at the back. ❧

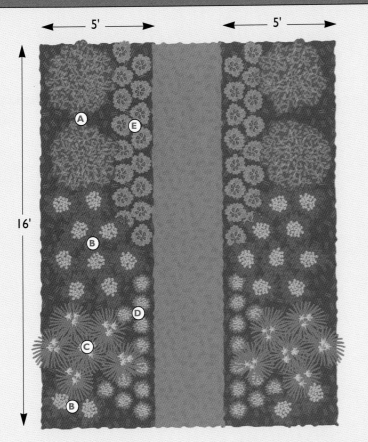

← 5' → ← 5' →

16'

PLANT LIST

A. Ligularia, 4, 4 to 6 feet tall

B. Bergenia, 22, 1 ½ feet tall

C. Daylily, 12 yellow,
     3 to 4 feet tall

D. Cypress spurge, 22, 1 foot tall

E. Bethlehem sage, 32, 1 foot tall

(See next page for more on plants.)

HERE'S HOW

CONTROLLING SLUGS

Shady, moist gardens are an ideal habitat for slugs. Feeding at night, slugs devour leaves, stems, bulbs, and fruits, leaving slimy trails of mucus as evidence of their presence. Here are two proven methods of control:

Place a board on the ground in your garden. Slugs will congregate underneath it overnight. Pick them off in the morning.

Fill a shallow pan with beer; sink it level with the soil surface. Slugs will fall in and drown. Empty frequently.

1. Measure a 5- x 16-foot border on either side of your walkway. Remove sod, till soil, add 3 to 4 inches of compost, and retill the soil.

2. Beginning at the back left, plant 2 ligularias (A) 3 feet apart, one in front of the other. (The planting beds on either side of the path are mirror images of each other. Plant one side first, then repeat on other side.)

3. Plant 9 bergenias (B) in 4 staggered rows in front of the ligularias, spacing plants and rows 18 inches apart. Plant 2 bergenias in the first, second, and fourth rows, and 3 in the third row.

4. Plant 6 daylilies (C) 18 inches apart in staggered rows in front of the bergenias with 2 in the first row, 3 in the second, and 1 in the third.

5. Plant 2 bergenias in front of the daylilies in a staggered row.

6. Plant 11 cypress spurges (D) 1 foot apart to the right of the daylilies and bergenias, as shown.

7. Plant 16 Bethlehem sages (E) in two staggered rows of 8 to the right of the ligularias and bergenias.

8. Repeat planting directions for right side. Mulch the gardens and water well.

Plants for Your Textured Walkway

The plants along this walkway are all suited to moist, shady conditions.

The texture of plants with dark foliage will be enhanced when placed between plants with lighter foliage. In shady areas of your garden, textured, dark-colored foliage tends to look flat and smooth because shadows are not well defined. Placing dark foliage beside lighter foliage makes the texture more noticeable. For example, the bergenia's distinct veining is more noticeable next to the gray-green of euphorbia than it is next to the dark green ligularia foliage.

Consider the texture of your walkway when planning your walkway garden. Here, concrete with an aggregate surface is a strong match for large-leaved plants and the various textures found in the planting. Other possibilities, depending on the character of your design, include pea gravel, wood bark, flagstones, or pavers. ❧

LIGULARIA
Ligularia przewalskii
4-6 feet tall
Zones 4-8
Yellowish, daisy-like flowers on arched spikes July to August; deeply lobed, rounded foliage; average to rich, moist soil; partial/full shade; medium/high water. Keep moist.

SIBERIAN BERGENIA (WINTER-BLOOMING BERGENIA)
Bergenia crassifolia
1½ foot tall
Zones 4-8
Rose-purple flowers February to April; glossy, leathery foliage, darker veins; average to rich, moist soil; partial sun/partial shade; medium/high water. Evergreen.

DAYLILY
Hemerocallis 'Hyperion'
3-4 feet tall
Zones 3-9
Yellow, trumpet-shaped flowers July to September; sword-shaped leaves; average to rich, moist soil; full sun/partial shade; medium water.

CYPRESS SPURGE
Euphorbia cyparissia,
1 foot tall
Zones 4-9
Yellow-green flowers May to June; rounded, shiny, gray-green leaves turn purplish red; average to rich, well-drained soil; full sun/partial shade; medium water.

BETHLEHEM SAGE (LUNGWORT)
Pulmonaria saccharata 'Mrs. Moon'
1 foot tall
Zones 4-8
Tubular flowers May to June open pink, turn blue; hairy, oval, pointed leaves with silvery spots; average to rich, moist soil; partial sun/full shade; medium water.

CARE FOR YOUR TEXTURED WALKWAY

SPRING Remove winter mulch, loosen soil between plants, and work organic matter into the soil. Trim back perennial growth remaining from last season and any ragged evergreen leaves. Mulch entire garden with a 3- to 4-inch layer of organic mulch.

SUMMER Remove spent flowers and trim plants where necessary to retain shape. Water garden regularly, especially during hot, dry periods. Remove aggressive cypress spurge plants, especially if they begin to hang over or grow onto the walk.

FALL Trim dead foliage to within 3 to 4 inches from the ground and compost healthy plants. Provide winter protection for all except evergreen plants by covering them with a noncompacting mulch. ❧

Alternative

A FRAGRANT WALKWAY

With a little bit of extra planning, you can create a garden walkway that is beautiful and fragrant as well as functional. The flowers or foliage of the perennial plants described here, when located along your walkway, will provide you with seasonal changes in perfume, color, and texture. Heartleaf crambe flowers, for example, envelop their large, coarse foliage in a light, airy mist of blooms that release a sweet scent. In a garden composed of a variety of scented plants, fragrances will replace one another as flowers bloom and fade. The aromatic foliage of artemisia and the flowering lavender will provide fragrance all season long when brushed against by passersby.

These plants need more sun and less moisture than do the plants for a textured walkway. A warm, sunny walkway will invigorate the fragrances that will, in turn, attract butterflies. However, you may want to trim back bee-attracting blossoms that are close to the walkway. Cool, misty mornings, days with high humidity, and warm evenings may change the intensity of fragrances.

Lavender and artemisia are commonly used to make potpourri and sachets. Their winter fragrances will remind you of summer strolls along your scented walkway.

CHOCOLATE COSMOS
Cosmos atrosanguineus
2 feet tall
Zones 6-10
Maroon, chocolate-scented, daisy-like blossoms on long, wiry stems July to September; branched stems with narrow, lance-shaped, dark green leaves; average, moist soil; full sun/partial shade; medium water. Remove faded flowers for continuous blooms. Good cut flower.

ENGLISH LAVENDER
Lavandula angustifolia **'Munstead'**
2 feet tall
Zones 5-9
Blue-violet, fragrant, tubular flowers on terminal spikes July to August; oval, gray-green foliage, evergreen in warmer climates; average, well-drained soil; full sun/partial shade; medium water. Very fragrant, even when dried.

ARTEMISIA (WORMWOOD)
Artemisia absinthium **'Lambrook Silver'**
3 feet tall
Zones 4-8
Inconspicuous flowers; aromatic, fine, deeply cut, silvery gray foliage; moist, poor to average, slightly alkaline, well-drained soil; full sun/partial shade; medium to low water. Trim back in spring for lush new growth.

HEARTLEAF CRAMBE (COLEWORT)
Crambe cordifolia
6 feet tall
Zones 6-9
Fragrant, white, star-shaped, small flowers in loose, airy clusters June to July; large, crinkly, lobed, deep green leaves; average, well-drained soil; full sun; medium water. Flowers can be dried, similar to baby's-breath.

TREE PEONY
Paeonia suffruticosa
4-5 feet tall
Zones 4-9
Pink, red, yellow, or white, fragrant, single to double flowers in June; deep green, veined, compound leaves with deeply cut lobes, sometimes tinged red or purple; average to rich, well-drained, moist soil; full sun/partial shade; medium water. Long-lasting cut flower.

An Inviting Entryway Garden

THIS GARDEN THRIVES WITH

SUN
Full

WATER
Medium

SOIL
Average

The most public part of your yard is the entrance. Planting an inviting, attractive garden creates a warm atmosphere that invites visitors right to your door. Depending on the plants used, visitors may be greeted by an array of vibrant colors or sweet scents.

Entrance gardens should have a more formal appearance than backyard gardens. Along a stone walk, a garden mulch of light-colored stone chips is preferable to straggly, shredded bark. Stray stone chips can be quickly swept back into the garden. They will also protect the plants from splashed soil particles or loose mulch when your garden is watered.

Privacy fences are a common feature of entrance gardens. They both define your personal space and act as a backdrop for the public part of your yard. If your entrance doesn't have a privacy fence, a sturdy trellis or an arbor can be substituted. Cover it with a climbing rose, and this feature will become the focal point of the garden, defining the limit of public space to your visitors. Choose a climbing rose that will bloom all season long and provide you with fragrance as well. Regardless of the maintenance they require, roses are popular, beautiful, and rewarding to grow. ❦

6'

12'

Using 18-inch spacing, plant 1 beard-tongue beside it and 4 beard-tongue around the maiden grass and 3 feet from its center.

6. Plant 6 coreopsis (E) along the walk, with the first plant placed 8 inches from the walk and 18 inches from the first beard-tongue. Space plants 1 foot apart. Plant a second row of 4 coreopsis behind the first row, staggering plants 1 foot behind and between the first 4 plants of the front row. Plant a third row of 3 coreopsis and a fourth row of 2 coreopsis.

7. Next, plant 2 Stoke's asters (F) 18 inches apart, at the back of bed and 18 inches between dwarf white pines. Plant 3 Stoke's asters 18 inches in front of first 2 asters. Plant remaining asters 18 inches to the left of the coreopsis, in two rows of 3 each. Stagger plants in each row for visual appeal.

8. Cover entire garden with 2 inches of compost. Cover compost with 2 inches of light-colored rock chip mulch. Water the garden thoroughly.

1. Clear an area 6 x 12-feet along your entrance walk. Till soil and spread 4 inches of compost over the surface. Retill the soil 6 inches deep.

2. Plant climbing rose (A) 10 inches from the fence and 3 feet from walk.

3. Plant maiden grass (B) 4 feet from the walk and 3 feet from the fence.

4. Plant 1 dwarf white pine (C) 5 feet from the fence and 5 feet in from the walk. Plant the other dwarf white pine 4 feet from the walk and 2 feet from the bottom edge of the garden.

5. Plant 1 beard-tongue (D) 1 foot from the fence and from the walk.

PLANT LIST

A. Climbing rose, 1, 8 to 10 feet tall

B. Maiden grass, 1, 5 to 6 feet tall

C. Dwarf white pine, 2, 3 to 8 feet tall

D. Beard-tongue, 6, 20 to 24 inches tall

E. Threadleaf coreopsis, 15, 18 to 24 inches tall

F. Stoke's aster, 11, 24 to 30 inches tall

(See next page for more on plants.)

HERE'S HOW

TRAINING CLIMBING ROSES

As your climbing rose grows, support the upper canes by training them to grow along a fence. You can purchase professional ties at a local nursery or use soft cloth or twine to fasten canes to the fence. Tie fasteners tight enough to support growing canes but not so tight as to strangle them. Never use wire or other rigid fasteners that can cut or sever canes.

Pleasing Plants for an Entryway

Mixing shrubs and perennials provides a permanent garden that will reward you year after year. Locate your entryway garden where it will receive full sun all day and where the soil is well drained. These plants all require regular watering. Enriching the soil with additional organic matter will help it retain moisture.

For larger flowers on your climbing rose, remove side buds 6 to 10 inches below the flower head prior to blooming. Faded blossoms should be cut off cleanly and at a slight angle. At season's end, trim canes to 2 feet and gently tie the lower canes together with cotton twine. Wrap stems with 4 to 6 layers of burlap and secure with twine. If your yard is regularly visited by deer or burrowing animals, create a wire cage around your rose. Bury bottom 3 to 6 inches deep and tightly secure the top to keep pests from feeding on the canes over winter. ❧

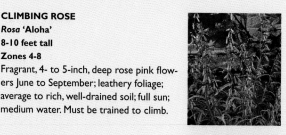

CLIMBING ROSE
Rosa 'Aloha'
8-10 feet tall
Zones 4-8
Fragrant, 4- to 5-inch, deep rose pink flowers June to September; leathery foliage; average to rich, well-drained soil; full sun; medium water. Must be trained to climb.

MAIDEN GRASS
Miscanthus sinensis 'Morning Light'
5-6 feet tall
Zones 5-10
Narrow, arching, green leaves with white margins; feathery blooms on 6-foot stems August to October; average, well-drained soil; full sun; medium water. Flowers can be dried.

DWARF WHITE PINE
Pinus strobus 'Nana'
3-8 feet tall
Zones 3-8
Blue-green to green, 3- to 5-inch needles on dense, irregular, bushy branches; average to rich, well-drained soil but tolerates dry, sandy conditions; full sun; medium water. Fast growing.

BEARD-TONGUE
Penstemon barbatus
20-24 inches tall
Zones 4-10
Spikes of 1-inch, rosy pink flowers June to August; glossy, oval foliage; average, well-drained soil; full sun; medium water. Remove faded blooms. Replace every 3 to 4 years.

THREADLEAF COREOPSIS
Coreopsis verticillata 'Moonbeam'
18-24 inches tall
Zones 4-10
Pale yellow, daisy-like flowers June to September; feathery, gray-green foliage; poor to average, well-drained soil; full sun; medium water. Remove faded blossoms. Divide every 2 to 3 years.

STOKE'S ASTER
Stokesia laevis 'Blue Danube'
24-30 inches tall
Zones 5-9
Purplish blue flowers August to October; silvery green leaves form mounding clumps; average, well-drained soil; full sun; medium water. Remove faded blooms. Heat tolerant.

CARE FOR YOUR INVITING ENTRYWAY GARDEN

SPRING Remove wrappings from rose and trim dead canes. Check fasteners. Retrain new shoots to maintain shape. Mulch the entire garden with 2 to 4 inches of organic mulch and cover again with stone chips. Trim new pine candles by half to reduce growth.

SUMMER Water garden regularly and remove faded blossoms. Cultivate soil and fertilize plants for increased flower production, especially for rose. Trim rose canes conforming to desired size and shape. Remove faded rose blossoms with clean cuts.

FALL Remove plant debris and compost healthy materials. Cut and prepare rose canes for the winter by wrapping them with burlap and wire. Cover perennials with a loose, noncompacting mulch held in place with evergreen boughs. ❧

Alternative

EASY CARE ENTRYWAY PLANTS

Low-maintenance plants require little attention during or after the growing season. They are capable of surviving dry, hot conditions with minimal watering and in general are pest- and disease-resistant. The low-maintenance perennials here need only to have the faded blossoms snipped off to maintain continuous flowering.

Climbing vines, such as five-leaf akebia, do not need special training, naturally wrapping themselves around their support. Simply thin lower stems, shorten branches, or snip dead twigs in spring for an attractive, trouble-free climber.

Hardy evergreen conifers such as the Chinese juniper provide interest during the winter months and serve as background plants during the growing season. They can be trimmed or pruned if too tall or leggy, but generally need little maintenance. Likewise, the billowing fountain grass and white coneflower seed cones will add interest to your entryway garden during even the coldest months. The plants in this low-maintenance garden provide an attractive, inviting entrance walkway with very little care.

CHINESE JUNIPER
Juniperus chinensis
4-5 feet tall
Zones 3-9
Small cones; silvery blue, dense needle-like foliage on arching stems, vase shaped; poor to average, well-drained soil; full sun; low water. Adaptable to most situations; does well in seaside areas.

FOUNTAIN GRASS
Pennisetum alopecuroides
3-5 feet tall
Zones 5-10
Soft, pinkish buff, 1-inch, feathery flowers above foliage August to October; dark green, narrow, coarse, arching leaves in a fountain shape; average, well-drained soil; full sun; low to medium water. Withstands drought.

JUPITER'S-BEARD (RED VALERIAN)
Centranthus ruber
2-3 feet tall
Zones 4-9
Dense clusters of fragrant crimson, pink, or white flowers atop strong stems June to July; gray-green leaves; poor to average, well-drained soil; full sun; low water. Remove faded flowers for continuous blooming. Extremely tolerant of heat and drought conditions.

FIVE-LEAF AKEBIA
Akebia quinata
12-15 feet tall
Zones 4-9
Fragrant, purplish flower clusters in spring followed by 3- to 4-inch, edible, purple fruits in September; blue-green, dense, compound leaves; poor to average, well-drained soil; full sun; low water. Twining growth attaches to support. Adapts to most situations. Minimal care.

WHITE CONEFLOWER
Echinacea purpurea **'White Swan'**
30-48 inches tall
Zones 3-9
Fragrant, 4- to 5-inch, daisy-like white flowers with orange or green centers June to September; oval, rough-textured foliage on brittle, branched stems; poor to average, well-drained soil; full sun; low to medium water. Seed cones for winter interest or dried arrangements.

A Petite Planting Around a Tree

THIS GARDEN THRIVES WITH

SUN

Part sun to shade

WATER

Medium

SOIL

Average, well drained

The right combination of plants can beautify the area surrounding a tree base with spectacular results. A little extra attention to planning and detail will give your landscape a finished look and provide an attractive focal point throughout the year. Creating a circular bed around a tree also eliminates the need to trim around the tree and will simplify lawn mowing.

The delicate, coordinated planting shown at left is only one part of this careful plan. In spring, lamium flowers enhance and balance this tree's pink blooms. Silvery lamium leaves will provide a distinctive contrast to the dark tree trunk all season as other plants bloom and fade. From early spring through fall, a succession of plants will appear.

Choose plants to match your growing conditions and to complement your tree's attributes, such as color and shape. If your climate is one with no snow cover, consider plants that are evergreen or have attractive seed pods for winter interest. Mulch and spreading ground covers can be attractive, low-maintenance alternatives to garden plants.

Ideally, you should install your garden around a tree when you plant the tree or shortly thereafter. It is difficult to cultivate or plant around established trees without damaging roots. 🌿

← 12' →

PLANT LIST

A. Lamium, 7, 4 to 10 inches tall

B. Lily of the valley, 25, 6 to 8 inches tall

C. Magic lily, 16, 2 to 3 feet tall

D. Hardy cyclamen, 36, 6 to 10 inches tall

(See next page for more on plants.)

HERE'S HOW

MICROWAVE DRYING PLANTS

1. Mark a circle 12 feet in diameter around a tree. Remove sod and till soil (be careful near roots). Add 2 inches of compost and till again.

2. Begin 2 feet in from the far edge and 3 ½ feet from the left side. Plant 2 lamiums (A) 3 feet apart. Closer to tree, offset a row of 3 lamiums 2 feet apart and, on the other side of the tree, another row of 2 lamiums.

3. One foot from the near side of garden edge, and 1 foot apart, plant a row of 3 lilies of the valley (B). Offset 2 rows of 6 and 8 behind this, spaced 1 foot apart. Plant 4 lilies of the valley in a square pattern on each side behind the end plants of the back row.

4. Plant the magic lilies (C) 4 inches deep and spaced 1 foot apart. Plant in 5 offset rows, beginning 4 feet from the far edge and 3 ½ feet from each side. Plant 1 in the first and last rows and 2 in the other rows.

5. Six inches from the edge of the bed, plant a ring of 36 cyclamens (D) 2 inches deep, spaced 1 foot apart.

6. Mulch the entire garden with 1 to 2 inches of organic mulch and water thoroughly.

Lily of the valley fragrance added to potpourri brings the scent of your garden indoors to last throughout the year. Prepare lily of the valley by cutting newly opened flowers just after the morning dew has dried. Place them between two sheets of paper towels and microwave on high for approximately 3 minutes, turning every 30 seconds until they feel dry and brittle. Store unused stalks in a covered glass jar.

Plants Around a Tree

Gardens under trees receive dappled shade for the hottest portion of the day. They get the most light in early morning and late afternoon, when the sun's angle is low. Plants in such a location must be able to tolerate these conditions. Shallow-rooted perennials work well since they don't need to be replaced each spring and offer little competition for tree roots.

Changing color and continual blooms keep this garden interesting all year. Lamium and lily of the valley start the season. During summer months, the silvery lamium foliage appears cool under the tree's green canopy. After other flowers have faded, the magic lilies appear with their dramatic pink flowers. Finally, the ring of cyclamen blossoms when few other plants are in bloom.

You can start the season even earlier by underplanting the cyclamens with blue Siberian squills and tucking tiny rock garden tulips in with lilies of the valley. 🌸

LAMIUM (DEAD NETTLE)
Lamium maculatum 'Beacon Silver'
4-10 inches tall
Zones 4-8
Pink flowers April to June above silvery white leaves with green margins on 3-foot spreading plants; average soil; partial sun/full shade; medium water. A tolerant, aggressive grower.

LILY OF THE VALLEY
Convallaria majalis
6-8 inches tall
Zones 3-9
Fragrant, tiny, white bell-shaped flowers May to June; deep green, spear-shaped, upright leaves; average, moist soil; partial sun/full shade; medium water. A pink-flowered variety is available.

MAGIC LILY
Lycoris squamigera
2-3 feet tall
Zones 5-9
Large pink flowers on tall, sturdy stems appear in August after green, strap-shaped foliage has disappeared in late spring; average, well-drained soil; full/partial sun; medium water.

HARDY CYCLAMEN (NEAPOLITAN CYCLAMEN)
Cyclamen hederifolium
6-10 inches tall
Zones 5-9
Flared pink flowers September to October; heart-shaped leaves; average to rich, well-drained, moist soil; partial/full shade; medium water.

GREIGII TULIP
Tulipa greigii
8-18 inches tall
Zones 3-8
Red with black and yellow at base, cup-shaped flowers from March to April; fleshy, basal, green leaves, mottled with purple; average, very well-drained soil; full sun; medium water.

SIBERIAN SQUILL
Scilla siberica
6-8 inches tall
Zones 3-9
One-inch, deep blue, bell-shaped flowers in March and April; narrow, strap-shaped, glossy green leaves in clumps; average, well-drained soil; full/partial sun; medium water.

CARE FOR YOUR GARDEN AROUND A TREE

SPRING Remove winter mulch. Fertilize garden if necessary, using care around tree roots, bulbs, and ground cover plants. Trim any low, broken, or hanging branches that block sunlight under the tree. Remove seed pods after bulbs flower.

SUMMER Water deeply during hot, dry weather: shallow watering causes tree roots to grow near surface and compete with other plants. Remove spent flowers and seed pods from summer-blooming bulbs. Trim yellowed bulb foliage at ground level.

FALL Allow plant foliage to die back naturally before trimming. If heavy leaf fall from tree blankets low-growing plants in bed, remove leaves, shred, and return a portion to the garden for winter mulch. Compost excess with other plant materials. 🌸

Alternative

LOW-GROWING PLANTS

Plantings under trees must tolerate both the tree's soil and moisture requirements. Junipers, carpet bugles, and wintercreepers are plants that grow in dry, poor soil, for example. If conditions are moist, try ferns, sweet woodruff, or wild ginger. Avoid planting under trees that produce growth-inhibiting chemicals. Norway maples and black walnuts, for example, produce toxins inhospitable to other plants. Planting in the deep shade under evergreen trees is also a special challenge.

Spreading plants and ground covers offer protection for tree roots by anchoring surface soil in place. In a mutually beneficial relationship, the leaves from deciduous trees will provide organic matter, enriching the soil for both the low-growing plants and the tree itself.

WILD GINGER
Asarum canadense
4-8 inches tall
Zones 4-9
Dark, bell-shaped ¾-inch-wide flowers below foliage April to May; 3- to 7-inch, medium green, heart-shaped leaves; average to rich, moist soil; full/partial shade; medium water. Strong-scented roots with a distinct gingery flavor. Native plant of North America.

SWEET WOODRUFF (BEDSTRAW)
Galium odoratum
1 foot tall
Zones 5-9
Small, airy, white, fragrant flowers May to June; fragrant, shiny green, narrow leaves forming star-shaped whorls; average to rich, moist, well-drained soil; full/partial shade; medium water. Foliage and flowers retain fragrance when dried. Repels insects in the garden and when dried.

CHRISTMAS FERN
Polystichum acrostichoides
1-2 feet tall
Zones 3-8
Dark green, shiny, lance-shaped leaves on slightly arching fronds forming a clump; evergreen; average to rich, moist soil; partial sun/full shade; medium to high water. With increased sun exposure, needs more organic matter in soil and more water.

CARPET BUGLE (BUGLE WEED)
Ajuga reptans 'Burgundy Glow'
4-8 inches tall
Zones 3-9
Blue flowers in terminal clusters above foliage April and May; colorful leaves mottled with green, white, pink, and purple; poor to average, well-drained soil; full sun/partial shade; low to medium water. Spreads by rooting where stems touch ground. Tolerant of hot, dry conditions.

CREEPING JUNIPER
Juniperus horizontalis 'Bar Harbor'
8-12 inches tall
Zones 3-9
Berry-like cones; bluish-gray, sharp needles on spreading branches up to 8-feet-long turn purplish in winter; poor to average, well-drained soil; full/partial sun; low to medium water. Tolerates dry, rocky conditions, including those at the seashore, as well as moist, acidic soils, Fast growing.

LITTLELEAF WINTERCREEPER
Euonymus fortunei 'Minima'
1-1 ½ feet tall
Zones 4-9
Shiny, dark green, oval leaves, ½ inch or less; poor to average, well-drained soil; full sun/partial shade; low to medium water. Tolerates dry or moist conditions. Numerous cultivars with variegated leaves, purplish tints, and different sizes. Remove stems that begin to climb trees.

A Fuss-Free Rock Garden

THIS GARDEN THRIVES WITH

SUN	WATER	SOIL
Full	Low to medium	Poor to average

Creating a rock garden can transform a bare slope or rock outcropping into a point of interest. Since rock gardens simulate alpine settings, they are uniquely suited to a slope or an embankment. An elaborate rock garden might contain features such as alpine shrubs, large boulders, waterfalls, or brooks. The fuss-free rock garden here can be built mostly by hand. If your site does not have large rocks, smaller ones can be positioned to look natural, especially when planted with tiny alpine flowers and shrubs.

Situate your rock garden on a sunny hillside or gentle slope. Or, place it near a stone patio or other permanent feature. Resist placing your rock garden under trees, where tree roots might be damaged or smothered.

Partially bury rocks to give the illusion of a ledge emerging from the soil. Expose more rock surface toward the garden front, which will create larger soil pockets for planting behind the ledge. Change elevation and tilt rocks for a more natural look.

Rock piles and larger stones of the same type are preferable to scattered rocks. Rocks with lichen and moss work best when placed weathered-side up. Rounded stones will give the illusion of a stream bed. 🌼

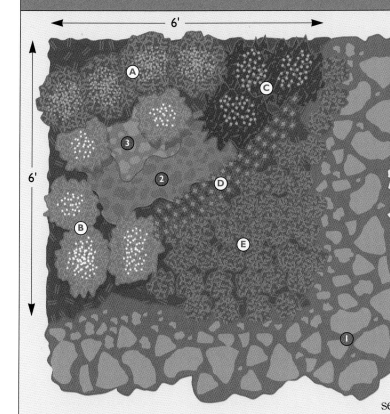

6'

6'

4. Plant 3 moss phlox (A) 1 foot apart, as shown, then 1 more, right of last phlox.

5. Plant 2 sedums (B), one on either side of rock area 3.

6. To right of phlox, plant 2 basket-of-golds (C) 1 foot apart, and 1 basket-of-gold offset 1 foot in front.

7. At front left corner of rock area 2, plant 3 sedums 1 foot apart as shown in diagram.

8. From front of rock area 2, extending to rock area 1 in a triangle, remove soil to 6-inch depth. In front of rock area 2, plant 3 rows of 16 tulips (D), as shown, with plants 4 inches apart. Mix soil with compost and carefully replace over the bulbs. Tamp with hands.

9. In remainder of triangle, with 6 inches between plants, plant rock cress (E) in front of tulip area. Offset rows back to front.

10. Using coarse rock chips, mulch the garden. Be careful not to injure small plants. Water well.

1. Choose a point at the top of the bank. Measure and mark a 6-foot square. Remove sod and soil to an 18-inch depth.

2. Beginning front left, construct stable rock area (1) along front and right sides. Place largest rocks outside, smaller rocks toward center. Construct two other, smaller rock areas (2 and 3) higher up, as shown in diagram.

3. Mix dug soil with coarse sand and gravel. Starting at front left, backfill behind rock area 1. Tamp and water soil every 4 inches to remove air pockets. Allow soil to settle 4 to 7 days, with final level 1 to 2 inches below area 1 rock surface.

PLANT LIST

A. Moss phlox, 4, 4 inches tall

B. Creeping sedum, 5, 2 inches tall

C. Basket-of-gold, 3, 1 foot tall

D. Tulip, 48 pink, 15 inches tall

E. Rock cress, 35, 2 inches tall

(See next page for more on plants.)

HERE'S HOW

A LEVEL- AREA ROCK GARDEN

Excavate the measured area to a depth of 18 inches. Set rocks aside. Mix soil with coarse sand and gravel to obtain well-drained consistency. Place 6 inches of coarse gravel in bed, arrange rocks in desired pattern on gravel. Backfill soil areas in 4-inch-layers, tamp, and water. Add extra soil over 4 to 7 days as settling occurs.

Fuss-Free Rock Garden Plants

Rock garden soil must be well drained. Weathering adds a constant supply of minerals and rock fragments to it. Rock chips form natural mulch, reducing runoff and erosion on soil that is thin and stony. Reproducing these conditions will help make your own rock garden fuss-free.

Rock garden plants are easy to grow and withstand wind and sun. Usually hardy, they may need mulch protection in northern climates where winter snow-cover is unreliable. In warm climates, rock gardens do better in low humidity. Choose plants appropriate to your region since growing alpine plants at different elevations, for example, will alter their performance and growth forms.

Rock gardening is akin to gardening in miniature. The low-growing plants, generally fine in texture, vary only inches in height. Some bloom or turn color in the fall, adding another season of pleasure in your garden. 🌿

MOSS PHLOX
Phlox subulata
4 inches tall
Zones 4-9
Star-shaped, pink flowers May to June; evergreen, mounding, needle-like, deep green foliage; average to sandy, well-drained soil; full sun; medium water. Spreads over rocks.

CREEPING SEDUM
Sedum spathulifolium **'Cape Blanco'**
2 inches tall
Zones 5-9
Star-shaped yellow flowers with green centers May to June; blue-green, fleshy leaves in small, flat rosettes; average to sandy, well-drained soil; full sun; medium water. Spreads 1 foot or more.

BASKET-OF-GOLD
Aurinia saxatilis
1 foot tall
Zones 4-7
Bright yellow, 4-petaled flowers with darker centers May to June; evergreen, oval, gray-green, hairy leaves; average, sandy, well-drained soil; full sun; medium water.

FOSTERIANA HYBRID TULIP
Tulipa **'Pink Perfection'**
12-18 inches tall
Zones 4-8
Pure pink, cup-shaped, single flowers March to early May, rising from center of fleshy, basal leaves; average to sandy, well-drained soil; full sun; medium water.

ROCK CRESS
Aubrieta deltoidea
2 inches tall
Zones 5-7
Violet-purple, single flowers May to June, yellow anthers; soft, mounding leaves; average to sandy, well-drained soil; full sun; medium water. Shear to remove faded flowers.

CARE FOR YOUR FUSS-FREE ROCK GARDEN

SPRING Carefully remove winter mulch. Remove stone-chip mulch from tulip area, add a 3-inch layer of compost, and replace stone chips. Add extra stone-chip mulch where it is sparse, in order to reduce weeds.

SUMMER Remove seed heads from faded tulips. Cut back yellowed tulip foliage. Water plants regularly if exposed to winds and warm temperatures. Shear plants to remove faded blossoms and to encourage growth. Trim long shoots and stems.

FALL Following frost, cut back dead stems and remove any plant debris. Compost healthy plant material. Cover entire garden with a nonpacking mulch such as straw. Cover mulch with evergreen boughs to hold it in place during the winter. 🌿

Alternative

A ROCK GARDEN FOR LEVEL SITES

If your site does not have a slope or a hill, you still can have a low-maintenance rock garden. Create your garden adjacent to a deck or patio, and add height through plant selection or by creating gentle slopes and mounds.

You may substitute an excavated site for a slope. You will want to build the center of your garden so that it is slightly higher than the outside edges to create a focal point and to improve drainage.

Varying plant heights can take the place of changes in elevation. Tall plants with interesting and unique foliage can provide a background for shorter plants. For example, the fern-like leaves and purple flowers of the Pasqueflower complement the delicate flowering rock soapwort.

In a level rock garden, you can use taller alpine shrubs as well as upright plants. Keep some rocks visible throughout the garden, even when plants are at their mature height. Vary foliage, texture, colors, times of bloom, and plant forms to create an individualized rock garden on a level site. ❦

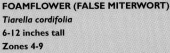

ROCK SOAPWORT
Saponaria ocymoides
1-6 inches tall
Zones 4-8
Numerous tiny, pink flowers with lighter centers June to July; hairy, oval leaves; average to poor, well-drained soil; full sun; low water. Water only when dry. Spreads and forms mat.

FOAMFLOWER (FALSE MITERWORT)
Tiarella cordifolia
6-12 inches tall
Zones 4-9
Numerous spikes of star-shaped, fluffy, white flowers May to June; spreading, lobed, pale green, dark-veined, maple-shaped leaves that turn deep red in fall; average to moist, well-drained soil; partial shade; low water. Water only when dry. Native wildflower.

DWARF CRANESBILL
Geranium sanguineum var. *prostratum*
6-10 inches tall
Zones 4-8
Many cup-shaped flowers, reddish purple to rose pink, June to August; mounding, spreading, deep green, deeply lobed foliage turning red in fall; average to moist, well-drained soil; full sun/partial shade; low water. Water only when dry.

PASQUEFLOWER
Anemone halleri
6-12 inches tall
Zones 5-7
Soft, 2 ½-inch, purple, cup-shaped flowers in April, forming feathery seed pods; soft, hairy, gray-green stems and fern-like leaves; average to poor, well-drained soil; full sun; low water. Water only when plant is dry.

JOHNNY-JUMP-UP (MINIATURE PANSY)
Viola tricolor
2-8 inches tall
Zones 3-8
Small, face-like blossoms in red, violet, yellow, purple, and combinations May to September; clump-forming, lobed, deep green foliage; average to moist, well-drained soil; full sun/partial shade; low water. Water only when dry; Remove faded blossoms to prevent seed production.

A Colorful Lamppost Planting

THIS GARDEN THRIVES WITH

SUN	WATER	SOIL
Full	Medium	Rich, well drained

Vertical features in your landscape, such as lampposts, mailboxes, signs, flagpoles, and lights, can be incorporated into your plantings to add interest and variety. By emphasizing your garden's horizontal lines, the height of vertical elements won't overwhelm their surroundings. The garden shown at left provides a good example. The plants do not obstruct light from the lamppost, but it becomes less prominent in the overall landscape design.

Repetition and contrast are elements often used in good garden design. Tall scarlet sage accents the repetitive white and purple color scheme along the front and side. Surrounding colors then subdue the sage's drama. Highlighted by the purple and white flowers in front, it is toned down by the reddish green leaves behind. The repetition of mounding plants, alyssum, and lobelia softens the pavement's edge, creating a graceful transition to the yard. The plants also flow onto the walk, reducing the straight division between garden and pavement.

Scarlet sage's vertical flower spikes mirror the upright lamppost while mounding alyssum and lobelia repeat the Japanese maple and mugo pine forms. Look for ways to use subtle repetition in your own lamppost or other plantings.

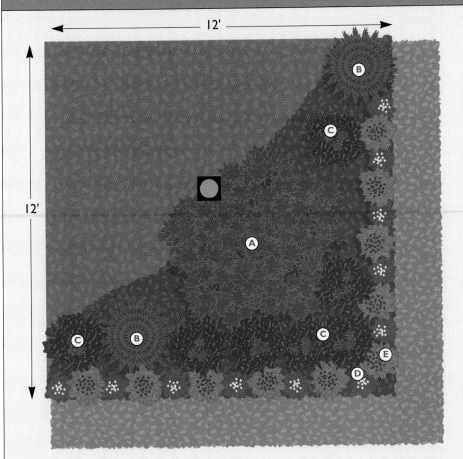

A. Japanese maple, 1, 6 to 8 feet tall

B. Mugo pine, 2, 3 to 4 feet tall

C. Scarlet sage, 7, 16 to 20 inches tall

D. Sweet alyssum, 11 white,
   6 to 12 inches tall

E. Lobelia, 10, 8 to 12 inches tall

(See next page for more on plants.)

HERE'S HOW

PLANTING A WINTER COVER CROP

Winter rye, oats, and vetch can grow in cold fall weather and add organic matter and nitrogen to the soil when turned under early in the spring. In fall, remove dead annuals, spread ½ inch of lime dust over the area, and till the soil 3 to 4 inches deep. Using a metal garden rake, level the soil and sprinkle with seed. Lightly rake the soil's surface with the rake's tines to set the seed. Till plants into soil in the spring when they are 2 to 3 inches tall, before seeds form.

1. Remove the sod from a triangular area with two equal sides of 12 feet. Till the soil, add a 4- to 6-inch layer of compost, and till again to a depth of 6 inches. Plant at same depth plants were in their containers.

2. Plant the Japanese maple tree (A) 6 feet from both front and right side of walk. Stake as in Here's How, page 119.

3. Plant 1 mugo pine (B), 8 feet left of front right corner, 2 feet from walk. Plant other mugo pine 10 feet from right corner at back, 2 feet from walk.

4. To the left of each pine, plant 1 scarlet sage (C) 30 inches in from garden edge. To the right of pine at left, plant 4 more 18 inches apart in a row, 30 inches from the garden's edge. Plant 1 more sage 18 inches above the last.

5. Spacing plants 1 foot apart and 6 inches in from the garden edges, alternate planting 11 alyssums (D) and 10 lobelias (E) along the two sides, beginning and ending with alyssums.

6. Cover the garden with 2 inches of compost. Top with 2 inches of shredded bark mulch. Water well.

Colorful Lamppost Blooms

Afront yard traditionally is given more formal treatment than the rest of a property. Mulching between plants evokes a formal appearance, while keeping down weeds and retaining moisture. Here, compost rich in nutrients has been spread over the garden and covered with shredded bark.

To compensate for lost nutrients in your annual plant area, you may want to sow a green cover crop into their beds in the fall (see Here's How, page 101). Your plants will respond with vigorous growth the next year.

When designing a lamppost garden, avoid taller trees that may block out lamplight. The low-growing Japanese maple and compact mugo pine unobtrusively accent the vertical lamppost. The circular mounding of the pine is repeated in the lobelia and alyssum. Remember to use caution when digging or tilling near buried electric lines that run to your lamppost. 🌺

JAPANESE MAPLE
Acer palmatum **'Dissectum Atropurpureum'**
6-8 feet tall
Zones 5-9
Reddish leaves turn rusty in fall; red, winged fruit in September; acidic, well-drained soil; full sun; medium water. Mounding; slow-growing.

COMPACT MUGO PINE (SWISS STONE PINE)
Pinus mugo **'Compacta'**
3-4 feet tall
Zones 2-7
Oval cones; needles form dense, circular mound; acidic, well-drained soil; full sun; medium water. Add compost. Buy only dwarf cultivars.

SCARLET SAGE
Salvia splendens **'Flare'**
16-20 inches tall
All zones
Scarlet spikes above foliage all summer; lance-shaped leaves; average, well-drained soil; full sun; medium water. Drought and heat tolerant. Attracts hummingbirds.

SWEET ALYSSUM
Lobularia maritima **'Snowcloth'**
6-12 inches tall
All zones
Fragrant, white flowers in clusters all summer; mounding, gray-green foliage; average, well-drained soil; full sun/light shade; water in dry weather. Shear to 3 inches after bloom.

LOBELIA
Lobelia erinus **'Crystal Palace'**
8-12 inches tall
All zones
Many small, deep purple-blue flowers all summer; deep bronzy green, mounding foliage; average to rich, well-drained soil; full sun; medium water. Enrich soil with compost.

CARE FOR YOUR COLORFUL LAMPPOST PLANTING

SPRING In annual area, till cover crop into soil for additional nutrients and organic matter. Add 2 to 4 inches of mulch to entire garden. After planting annuals, mulch entire area with 2 inches of shredded bark.

SUMMER Water garden regularly, including trees and shrubs. Remove spent flowers from annuals, and shear alyssums to encourage repeat bloom.

FALL Remove and compost dead, healthy annual plants after the first frost. Dispose of any diseased plants away from the garden. Maple leaves can be left under trees as they will decompose and add natural nutrients to soil. 🌺

Alternative

A COLORFUL LOW-MAINTENANCE LAMPPOST PLANTING

Plants that prefer dry, hot conditions will thrive with only minimal feeding and watering during the growing season. Shearing the spent blossoms of verbena is an easy way to promote continuous blooms all summer long. Snip faded globe amaranth flowers for quick, easy maintenance, or cut for fresh or dried arrangements. None of these plants require continual care, so a quick snip here and there will have them looking great in no time.

The plants and surroundings of this low-maintenance garden suggests the use of particularly suitable material for mulching. In the dry Southwest, try using light-colored stone chips as a mulch. In hot, dry climates, moisture in the air collects on stones during the night, trickling between cracks and spaces to reach the soil. Light color also reflects the sun, keeping the soil below cooler and more likely to retain precious moisture. Because light-colored stone chips are similar in both coloring and texture to the walkway, the distinction between the pavement and the garden is reduced further. A quick sweep over the pavement will send stray rock chips back into the mulch. You'll be able to sit back and enjoy the compliments you'll get on your colorful, low-maintenance planting. 🌺

SMALL SOAPWEED
Yucca glauca
3-4 feet tall
Zones 5-10
Fragrant, 3-inch, waxy, white, pendulous flowers on 3- to 4-foot stalks July to August; narrow, spear-shaped, gray-green leaves with white margins and white threads, forming a circular clump; poor to average, well-drained, dry soil; full sun; low water. Withstands heat and drought.

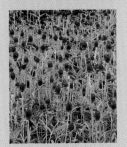

GLOBE AMARANTH
Gomphrena globosa **'Strawberry Fields'**
20-24 inches tall
All zones
Bright red, clover-shaped flowers on long stems all summer when faded blossoms removed; deep green, bushy foliage; poor to average, well-drained, dry soil; full sun; low water. Tolerates heat and drought. Stake plants in windy areas. Long-lasting cut flower; dried flowers retain bright color.

GARDEN VERBENA
Verbena x hybrida **'Blue Lagoon'**
8-12 inches tall
All zones
Deep blue or white, 2- to 3-inch, flat flower clusters on wiry stems all summer when spent blooms removed; gray-green, stiff, hairy leaves on dense, mounding plants; poor to average, well-drained, dry soil; full sun; low water. Tolerates heat and drought.

CHASTE TREE
Vitex Agnus-castus **'Alba'**
8-10 feet tall
Zones 6-10
Fragrant, thin racemes of white flowers 8 to 12 inches long, August to September; 5 to 7 deep green, aromatic, compound leaflets 2 to 5 inches long; mounding, arching form; poor to average, well-drained, dry soil; full sun; low water. Thrives in hot, dry conditions.

A Moisture-Loving Garden

THIS GARDEN THRIVES WITH

SUN	WATER	SOIL
Part to full shade	High	Average to rich

Don't let the perpetually wet spots in your yard intimidate you. These areas can be transformed into spectacular, moisture-loving gardens. There are many plants that can tolerate or even require boggy conditions in order to thrive. If you do not have an area that is naturally wet but would like to grow plants that are moisture-loving, a marsh garden is easy to construct (see Here's How, page 105).

Moisture-loving gardens are best in areas that naturally retain water—miniature wetlands. In these wetlands, you can grow plants that won't thrive under other conditions, for instance the bog garden candelabra primroses. Bog gardens placed next to ponds can provide attractive transitions to the rest of the garden and, in late summer when other garden plants may not be at their most attractive, your moisture-loving plants will look delightfully fresh.

You will want to place a raised path, steppingstones, or rocks nearby from which to view your garden without crushing plants or stepping in water. Check water level regularly during the growing season, adding water if necessary. Marsh gardens are very difficult to overwater. ❧

6'

4'

PLANT LIST

A. Candelabra primrose, 6, 2 feet tall

B. Siberian iris, 1, 2 ½ feet tall

C. Astilbe, 4, 2 feet tall

D. Japanese sedge, 6, 2 feet tall

(See next page for more on plants.)

HERE'S HOW

CONSTRUCTING A MARSH GARDEN

1. Measure a 4- x 6-foot area in your garden wetland. Remove sod and stones. In the wettest spot, dig a shallow depression 4 to 10 inches lower than the surrounding soil, to hold open water. Place a large rock at the garden's edge, next to the depression.

2. Till soil to a depth of 1 foot. Add 6 to 8 inches of compost to the surface and retill to a depth of 4 to 6 inches. Plants should be at same depth they were in their nursery containers.

3. Beginning near water as shown, plant 5 primroses (A) 1 foot apart near rock and along water's edge.

4. Plant 1 iris (B) 18 inches from the right garden edge and 2 feet behind the primroses.

5. Plant the astilbes (C) in a triangle, as shown, 2 feet apart and 1 foot from the back garden edge.

6. Beginning at the back left corner of the garden, plant 4 Japanese sedges (D) 1 foot apart in a row coming forward. Plant 2 more, 1 foot to the right of first row, and 1 foot apart, as shown.

7. Plant 1 primrose at left, between the Japanese sedges and the edge of the water.

8. Mulch the garden with 4 to 6 inches of compost and water well to settle plant roots.

Dig an area 18 inches deep in sun or part shade. Line with 2 inches of sand, and place a 40-mil black plastic liner (available from pond supply catalogs or garden supply stores) over the sand. Cut drainage holes in the liner 8 inches from top. Fill liner with soil high in organic matter. Make a depression in the soil to allow for a pool of standing water, if desired. Water until the soil is completely saturated and the low area is full of water. Set stones around edge for an attractive look.

Pretty Plants for Wet Sites

Moisture-loving plants vary in their growing requirements. Some prefer to be continually moist, while others like standing in water.

Try planting astilbe and Siberian iris in any wet, low-lying areas of your garden. Experiment until you find the right plants for your wet site. If your natural garden soil is too well drained for moisture-loving plants, try growing them in pots. Add extra organic matter (or vermiculite) to the potting soil to increase moisture retention and keep your plants well watered.

If you plan to construct a marsh garden, choose a site that suits your moisture-loving plants. If you garden in the South, most plants will need a partially shaded area out of the hot summer sun. In northern areas with high humidity, part to full sun is acceptable with a constant supply of water. If you live in a dry climate, partial sun is best for these plants.

ASTILBE
Astible x *arendsii* **'Snowdrift'**
2 feet tall
Zones 4-8
Feathery white flowers June to August; finely cut, deep green foliage; slightly acidic soil; in the South, plant in shade; in the North, plant in partial shade; keep moist.

SIBERIAN IRIS
Iris siberica **'Shirley Pope'**
2 ½ feet tall
Zones 5-9
Large purple blooms June to July; narrow green leaves; acidic soil; in South, plant in shade; in North, prefers partial shade; in sun, tolerates continuously moist, boggy soil.

JAPANESE SEDGE
Carex morrowii **'Goldband'**
1-2 feet tall
Zones 5-8
Deep green, white-edged, arching blades; average soil, tolerates standing water up to 4 inches; in South, plant in shade; in North, partial shade, full sun if kept moist.

CANDELABRA PRIMROSE
Primula prolifera
2 feet tall
Zones 4-8
Yellow clusters of flowers rising 1 foot above foliage April to May; slightly acid soil; in South, plant in shade; in North, partial shade but will tolerate full sun if kept moist.

CARE FOR YOUR MOISTURE-LOVING GARDEN

SPRING Cultivate around perennial plants to loosen soil and improve aeration. Avoid compacting waterlogged soil. Apply compost to the garden surface and work into soil; add more compost or other organic mulch to the soil surface to smother weeds and keep water from evaporating.

SUMMER Water plants regularly during the growing period, especially if weather is hot and dry. Mulch with additional organic matter to supply necessary nutrients and retain as much moisture as possible. Trim dead blossoms prior to seed formation for healthier, more productive plants the following year.

FALL Cut back dead foliage to 6 inches after first frost to discourage diseases and pests the following year. Cover plants with 6 inches of healthy plant trimmings and compost any leftover, healthy trimmings. Drain standing water from plants by deepening the depression in your garden or by using a siphon.

Alternative

FOLIAGE PLANTS FOR A MOISTURE-LOVING GARDEN

Foliage plants can provide interest all season long without waiting for flower blossoms. They are available in a wide range of textures, colors, and shapes. In some cases, the flowers of foliage plants are insignificant, while others have blooms that are a wonderful bonus.

Soil must never be allowed to dry out in any moisture-loving garden. Check the water level regularly, especially during hot, dry weather, and add water as needed. Nearby drier soils will draw moisture out of your marsh garden. Use gravity to help you regulate the amount of water each plant receives. Place plants that need more water in the lowest areas, where water collects, and those that need less water in higher, drier places.

You can add natural features around the edges of your moisture-loving garden to lessen the abrupt change from the surrounding site. Using props such as rocks, weathered wood, and gravel can ease the transition between boggy areas and other parts of your garden. A pile of large, flat stones can help to form a watering place where soil and plants are not dislodged. Simply wedge or anchor the hose so the water runs across the rocks, slowing its force. 🌿

VARIEGATED YELLOW FLAG (YELLOW IRIS)
Iris pseudacorus 'Variegata'
4-5 feet tall
Zones 3-9
Yellow flowers with purple veins and markings May to June; sword-shaped, long, narrow foliage with yellow edges; very moist, acidic, organic soils; in South, plant in shade; in North, prefers partial shade but will tolerate full sun if kept very moist; naturalized iris found in waterways.

HOUTTUYNIA
Houttuynia cordata 'Chameleon'
12-15 inches tall
Zones 5-9
White flowers on red stalks June to July; multicolored markings on deep green, heart-shaped leaves; wet or very moist soil; in South, plant in shade; in North, prefers partial shade but tolerates full sun if kept very moist; high water. More sun produces greater leaf variegation.

BLUE HOSTA (PLANTAIN LILY)
Hosta ventricosa 'Aureo-marginata'
12-18 inches tall
Zones 4-9
Violet flowers on stalk above foliage July to August; mound of 8-inch, green, heart-shaped leaves with wavy edges and irregular, light margins; average to rich, moist soil enriched with organic matter; in South, plant in shade; in North, prefers partial shade but will tolerate full sun if kept very moist.

ROYAL FERN
Osmunda regalis
3-4 feet tall
Zones 3-8
Dense, glossy, deep green fronds with rounded leaflets, tips of fronds bronzy pink and almost flower-like; moist or wet soils with high organic matter; in South, plant in shade; in North, prefers partial shade but will tolerate full sun if kept very moist; high water.

Designing for a Special Style

How do you go about deciding on a personal garden style? The first step is to ask yourself why you want a garden—what will be its purpose? There are many possible answers. The designs in this section were chosen to help you find a style that satisfies your needs and expresses your preferences.

You will want to consider where your garden is going to be and make sure the style you have in mind can be adapted to your site. You may find that the architecture of your home or the character of your neighborhood is best suited to a specific kind of garden. A good garden design will create a unified outdoor atmosphere that will also fit your surroundings and mode of life.

Identify what makes a distinctive garden style appealing to you. Do you prefer the variety of a cottage garden, the hardiness of a native garden, or the fragrance of a rose garden? Gourmet cooks may want to plant an herb garden not only for its charm but also for its utility.

Think about what attracts you to a garden most: color, fragrance, shape? You can give distinction to a common style by incorporating your preferred variations. As you review the varieties of garden styles presented in this section, you will see that the possibilities are endless. You can adapt the garden projects here to develop your own particular theme. You will quickly discover the excitement of expressing your special style through garden design. ❧

A Classic Cottage Garden

THIS GARDEN THRIVES WITH

SUN
Full

WATER
Medium

SOIL
Average, well drained

Cottage gardens are informal, colorful medleys of annuals, shrubs, perennials, and sometimes herbs and vegetables as well. Originally grown for a family's medicinal and culinary needs, cottage gardens remind us of the country gardens of the past.

As you plan your cottage garden, consider any natural features already in place, such as large rocks, fruiting shrubs, vines, or trees. Trellises, birdbaths, swings, benches, and fences also can become a part of your cottage garden design. The plants at left grow through the railings and billow over the top of a picket fence for a natural, uncontrived look.

Cottage gardens are generally low maintenance, requiring only weeding and the removal of spent flowers to keep them looking their best. Choose a sunny location and prepare your soil well. Cultivate carefully around established perennials and volunteer plants that spring up from self-sowing annuals or perennials, such as pansies and foxgloves. Thin the seedlings but allow a few to grow randomly for a casual, cottage garden effect.

4'

4'

20'

PLANT LIST

A. Hybrid tea rose, 2, 4 to 5 feet tall

B. Delphinium, 1 white, 1 purple, 1 pink, 4 to 6 feet tall

C. Foxglove, 2 purple, 1 pink, 1 white, 3 to 6 feet tall

D. Strawflower, 6 pink, 3 white, 1 foot tall

E. Dusty miller, 5, 1 to 2 feet tall

(See next page for more on plants.)

1. Remove the sod from areas 4 x 20 feet on both sides of a picket fence. Till soil, add 2 to 3 inches of compost, and retill the soil.

2. On the back side of the fence, plant 2 roses (A), one 3 feet from the left edge and the other 7 feet to the right of the first.

3. Plant 2 delphiniums (B), 1 dark purple between the roses and a pink one 3 feet to the right of the second rose.

4. Plant 1 purple foxglove (C) 2 feet to the right of the pink delphinium.

5. Plant 3 foxgloves in front of the picket fence: 1 purple 4 feet from the left, 1 pink 4 feet away from the purple, and 1 white 1 ½ feet in from the right side of the garden.

6. In front of the fence, plant the remaining white delphinium between the pink and white foxgloves.

7. Plant groups of 3 strawflowers (D) beginning on the left side with 3 white, then 3 pink between the pink foxgloves and the white delphinium, and another pink group between the white delphinium and white foxglove.

8. Plant a group of 3 dusty millers (E) between the purple and pink foxgloves, and 1 dusty miller behind the fence as shown.

9. Water thoroughly and mulch the entire garden with an organic mulch such as compost or wood chips.

HERE'S HOW

WIRING STRAWFLOWERS

Wire strawflowers for winter display by removing all but ½ inch of the stem. Using an 8- to 12-inch piece of florist wire, push it up through the stem and 1 inch above the flower top. Bend the 1-inch wire end to form a U (upside down) approximately ½ inch long and pull long wire back down until the U disappears. Hang upside down in a cool, dry, shady place until dry, then wrap the wire stem with green florist tape.

Classic Cottage Garden Flowers

Cottage gardens depend primarily on a mixture of old-fashioned plants for their charm. These gardens are a link to the abundant and varied plantings of the past. The casual, bountiful effect of a cottage garden is achieved by choosing a variety of plant shapes and colors, and by combining heights and textures.

Roses are a staple of the old-fashioned cottage garden. They perfectly suit the traditional look of the picket fence in this cottage garden design. The color of the 'Peace' rose is repeated in plants of varying forms and heights, such as the low-growing pink and white strawflower and the tall, rosy spires of foxglove. Intermittent white variations accent the garden. The subtle silvery white foliage of dusty miller anchors the bed to the earth and helps harmonize the other garden plants with the delightful roses that will bloom throughout most of the summer. ❧

HYBRID TEA ROSE
Rosa 'Peace'
4-5 feet tall
Zones 5-9
Pink-and-yellow, fragrant, 4- to 6-inch flowers June to August; glossy, dark blue-green, bushy foliage; average to rich, well-drained soil; full sun; medium water. Remove spent blooms.

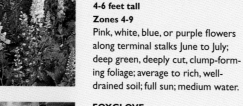

DELPHINIUM
Delphinium elatum 'Magic Fountains'
4-6 feet tall
Zones 4-9
Pink, white, blue, or purple flowers along terminal stalks June to July; deep green, deeply cut, clump-forming foliage; average to rich, well-drained soil; full sun; medium water.

FOXGLOVE
Digitalis purpurea
3-6 feet tall
Zones 4-9
Purple, pink, or white tubular flowers along terminal stalks June to July; rosettes of shiny, green leaves; average to rich, well-drained soil; partial sun/partial shade; average water. Self-sowing biennial.

STRAWFLOWER
Helichrysum bracteatum
'Bright Bikini Mix'
1 foot tall
All zones
Pink and white, stiff, papery flowers all summer; coarse, green foliage; average to rich, well-drained soil; full sun; medium water. Popular dried.

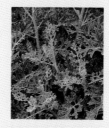

DUSTY MILLER
Senecio cineraria
1-2 feet tall.
All zones
Insignificant yellow-white flowers; velvety, stiff, finely cut, silvery white foliage; average, well-drained soil; full sun/partial shade; low to medium water. Remove tiny flowers.

CARE FOR YOUR COTTAGE GARDEN

SPRING Remove protective winter mulches. Thin volunteer seedlings and add new plants to the garden. Mulch open areas to keep weeds to a minimum. Incorporate 1 to 2 inches of organic matter into the soil, especially around roses and other heavy feeders.

SUMMER Water your garden regularly and remove spent flowers to extend bloom periods. Trim annuals to keep them bushy and flowering. Stake taller plants or loosely tie stems or stalks to fence. Allow annuals and perennials to form seed late in the season.

FALL Shake dried seed pods to distribute seed, and cut back tops of dead perennials. After ground has frozen, cover perennials with noncompacting mulch, such as straw, for winter protection, and mound earth around the bases of rose plants. ❧

Alternative

A WHITE COTTAGE GARDEN

Single-color cottage gardens with old-fashioned flowers can also be charming. Use a single color to blend with a dominant element, perhaps by creating a white garden along a stretch of white picket fence. Selecting a particular color, perhaps that of your house's trim, and using it for all of your garden plants can be surprisingly delightful. And if you have a garden element, such as a vibrant red clematis vine, that you especially love, surround it with an informal grouping of white-flowering plants as a frame.

When choosing plants for a single-color garden, pay particular attention to texture, size, and shape. Separate large areas of the same color by using foliage plants, leafy shrubs, or neutral elements. Plant shorter annuals in front of bushy, taller plants. If you balance your planting by staggering the flowering times of perennials and shrubs, you will create the impression of white through-out the garden for the entire season. 🌿

SNAPDRAGON
Antirrhinum majus 'White Sonnet'
2 ½-3 feet tall
All zones
Two-lipped, white flowers along terminal spikes all summer; lance-shaped, green foliage; average to rich, well-drained soil; full sun; medium water. Remove faded flowers for continuous blooms. Long-lasting cut flower.

SO SWEET HOSTA (PLANTAIN LILY)
Hosta 'So Sweet'
2 feet tall
Zones 3-9
White, very fragrant, bell-shaped flowers on a stalk just above foliage in July; large, green, heart-shaped leaves with white margins; average to rich, moist soil; partial sun/full shade; medium to high water.

HYBRID TEA ROSE
Rosa 'Pascali'
4 feet tall
Zones 5-9
Double, 3- to 4-inch, fragrant, creamy white flowers and buds all season; deep green, oval, shiny leaves with serrated edges; average to rich, well-drained, moist soil; full sun; medium water.

GARDEN PHLOX
Phlox paniculata 'Mount Fuji'
3-4 feet tall
Zones 2-8
Fragrant, pure white, terminal flower clusters June to September; lance-shaped, green leaves with distinct midrib; average to rich, moist soil; full sun/partial shade; medium water. Give plants adequate spacing to prevent mildew.

HOLLYHOCK
Alcea rosea 'Chater's Double White'
5-7 feet tall
Zones 3-8
Double, 3- to 5-inch, white flowers along terminal spikes from June to frost; 4- to 8-inch, dark green, rounded leaves; average, well-drained soil; full sun; medium water. Needs to be staked only in windy sites.

An All-American Rose Garden

THIS GARDEN THRIVES WITH

SUN
Full

WATER
Medium

SOIL
Average to rich, well drained

Roses have aptly been called the "Queen of Flowers." Their glorious blooms and extravagant fragrances have made them romantic favorites, cultivated for thousands of years and handed down from generation to generation. Settlers brought rose slips with them not just for their beauty but as a basic necessity of life. Household roses were used for sachets, to flavor cakes and jams, and even for medicinal purposes as they provided vitamin C with their rose hips.

More types of roses are constantly being added to old favorites, and recently emphasis has been on everblooming, large-flowered hybrid teas. This garden is planned with hybrid teas spaced in single rows to provide the air circulation that will keep disease and insect infestations to a minimum.

An edging of low-growing wax begonias hides the open bases of the hybrid teas. The begonias give a finished look to the beds and repeat the white color of the 'John F. Kennedy' rose. The color of the 'Mr. Lincoln' red is repeated in the striking floribunda roses planted in front of the arbor. Although at left you see a clematis climbing over the arches, for an even more spectacular entranceway you may want to plant a red 'Don Juan' climbing rose instead. ❀

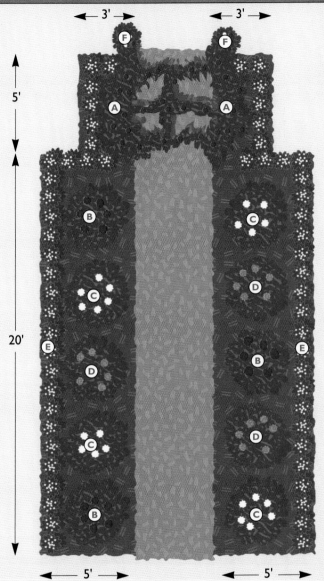

PLANT LIST

A. Climbing rose, 2 red,
12 to 14 feet tall

B. Hybrid tea rose, 3 red, 4 feet tall

C. Hybrid tea rose, 4 white,
3 feet tall

D. Hybrid tea rose, 3 pink, 4 feet tall

E. Wax begonia, 60 white, 1 foot tall

F. Floribunda rose, 2 red and white
striped, 3 to 4 feet tall

(See next page for more on plants.)

3. Plant a row of hybrid tea roses 2 feet in from the walk and spaced 4 feet apart: 1 red (B), 1 white (C), 1 pink (D), 1 more white, and 1 more red.

4. Plant an opposite row of hybrid tea roses: 1 white, 1 pink, 1 red, 1 pink, and 1 white—again planting them 2 feet away from the middle walk and spacing them 4 feet apart.

5. On each side of the rose beds, along the outside edges, plant 20 wax begonias (E) behind the hybrid tea roses and a row of 6 wax begonias behind the climbing roses. Plant 2 wax begonias between these two rows, and 1 in front of the ends of each row of 6, as shown.

6. Plant 1 floribunda rose (F) on each side of the arbor entryway.

7. Mulch the entire garden with 2 to 3 inches of organic mulch, such as wood chips, and water thoroughly.

1. Mark and prepare areas 5 x 20 feet on both sides of the walk and 3 x 5 feet on both sides of the arbor. Remove sod, till the soil, add 4 to 6 inches of compost, and retill the soil.

2. Plant 1 climbing rose (A) centered on each side of the arbor and 1 foot away from arbor.

HERE'S HOW

PROPAGATING ROSES BY LAYERING

Select a flexible, healthy cane 1 foot or longer. Remove foliage from the bottom half. Three to four inches up the stem, cut a 1-inch-long, ¼-inch-deep slit. Leave stem intact, wedge the slit open with a toothpick and bury it in a trench 2 to 4 inches deep. Next spring, separate cane from original plant, dig up the newly rooted stem, and transplant to its permanent location.

A Radiant Rose Garden

This all-American garden features the dark red, richly perfumed 'Mr. Lincoln', legendary throughout the rose world. 'Scentimental' follows an American tradition of striped roses dating back to the 1800s. The white 'John F. Kennedy' rose was named to memorialize a slain president, and 'Dainty Bess', with its continuously blooming pure pink flowers, is one of the best old-fashioned hybrids. Even the colorful 'Don Juan' was bred in the United States. These roses, when located in full sun and well cared for, will respond with magnificent blooms all summer.

Roses are best acquired bare-root and fully dormant in early spring. Plant them in moist soil generously enriched with organic matter. Water well until the plants are established. Your roses will benefit from light cultivation and regular fertilization throughout the season. 🌸

CLIMBING ROSE
Rosa 'Don Juan'
12-14 feet tall
Zones 5-9
Deep red, fragrant, 3- to 5-inch, double roses in clusters all season; green leaves with serrated edges; average to rich, well-drained, moist soil; full sun; medium water. Long canes need to be tied and trained.

HYBRID TEA ROSE
Rosa 'Mr. Lincoln'
4 feet tall
Zones 6-9
Dark red, very fragrant, velvety, 4-inch flowers all season; deep green, shiny leaves with serrated edges; average to rich, well-drained, moist soil; full sun; medium water. Impressive long-stemmed cut flower.

HYBRID TEA ROSE
Rosa 'John F. Kennedy'
3 feet tall
Zones 5-9
Pure white, large, double, fragrant flowers all season, with raised centers; deep green, oval, shiny leaves with serrated edges; average to rich, well-drained, moist soil; full sun; medium water. Prolific bloomer.

HYBRID TEA ROSE
Rosa 'Dainty Bess'
4 feet tall
Zones 5-9
Pure pink, 3- to 4-inch, single flowers all season, with yellow stamens; green, shiny leaves with serrated edges; average to rich, well-drained, moist soil; full sun; medium water.

WAX BEGONIA
Begonia semperflorens 'Victory White'
8-12 inches tall
All zones
Satiny white, small, 4-petaled flowers all summer; waxy, bronze or green, rounded leaves on brittle stems; average, well-drained soil; full sun/partial shade; medium water.

FLORIBUNDA ROSE
Rosa 'Scentimental'
3-4 feet tall
Zones 5-9
Red and white, multipetaled 4-inch flowers all season; quilted leaves; average to rich, well-drained, moist soil; full sun; medium water. Upright, rounded growth. Strong fragrance.

CARE FOR YOUR ROSE GARDEN

SPRING Remove protective winter mulch and cultivate 3 inches of compost into the soil. Trim canes back to 6 to 12 inches. Prepare border soil for annuals by incorporating compost. Feed roses with a liquid fertilizer specifically formulated for roses.

SUMMER Continue feeding your roses regularly. Clip faded blossoms and check for insects or disease. Remove and discard any diseased plant materials. If necessary, spray roses with a soap solution to smother sucking insects.

FALL After killing frost, trim back longest canes for the winter. Mound soil around the base of the roses and encircle them with a wire cylinder 2 to 3 feet high, filled with non-compacting organic mulch. Use a small wire mesh to keep animals out. 🌸

Alternative

A DAYLILY GARDEN

Daylilies are easier to grow than roses and fun to collect. They show a great range of colors and, besides the typical trumpet shape, there are many unusual petal forms. Choose from narrow, twisted, or ruffled petals, with single or double flowers up to 10 inches across. Daylilies vary in height from 1 to 5 feet, with some that show brilliantly in the landscape and others that are remarkably subtle up close. They can be planted in an informal design or in formal settings, forming dense clumps that need little care. Daylilies are amazingly hardy and will tolerate both wet and dry soil. They are excellent border plants and will thrive in difficult terrain, such as on steep slopes. Daylilies are also very easy to propagate, making them a good choice for spacious garden areas.

The flowers are borne on top of strong stems, with a cluster of buds that open over a period of time. Each bud remains open just one day, hence the name daylily. Most plants are capable of producing up to 30 flowers in one season and can bloom over a period of 1 to 3 months. You will find them a constant joy in your summer garden. ❧

DAYLILY
Hemerocallis 'Gentle Shepherd'
2-3 feet tall
Zones 4-9
Ivory white, trumpet-shaped flowers with chartreuse green throats, June to July; dark green, narrow, sword-shaped foliage; average to rich, moist soil; full sun/part shade; medium water.

DAYLILY
Hemerocallis 'Rainbow Round'
1 ½ -2 feet tall
Zones 4-9
Silvery pink, satiny, trumpet-shaped flowers with yellow throats, July to August; dark green, narrow, sword-shaped foliage; average to rich, moist soil; full sun/part shade; medium water.

DAYLILY
Hemerocallis 'Little Sweet Sue'
16-18 inches tall
Zones 3-9
Deep red, trumpet-shaped, 3-inch flowers with green throats, June to July; dark green, narrow, sword-shaped foliage; average to rich, moist soil; full sun/part shade; medium water.

DAYLILY
Hemerocallis 'Hyperion'
3 ½ -4 feet tall
Zones 4-9
Lemon yellow, trumpet-shaped, fragrant flowers July to September; dark green, narrow, sword-shaped foliage; average to rich, moist soil; full sun/part shade; medium water.

DAYLILY
Hemerocallis 'Stella de Oro'
14-16 inches tall
Zones 4-9
Golden yellow, trumpet-shaped, 3- to 4-inch flowers July to frost; dark green, narrow, sword-shaped foliage; average to rich, moist soil; full sun/part shade; medium water. Prolific repeat bloomer. One of the best.

A Native Plant Garden

THIS GARDEN THRIVES WITH

SUN

WATER

SOIL

Full to partial   **Medium to high**   **Average to rich**

Interest in native plant gardens has grown dramatically over the past few years. What began as a search for a more environmentally friendly—as well as a less work-intensive—approach to landscaping and gardening has developed into a rediscovery of the beauty and variety that native plants have to offer. Native plants are easily cared for because they flourish in their local habitats—an added incentive to explore your own native garden possibilities.

Conditions in your landscape and garden will help you decide which plants to choose. Start by determining which areas of your garden are sunny, shaded, exposed to winds, sheltered, low and wet, or high and dry. Test your soil to determine type and water content.

With this information in mind, observe natural areas in your region and note plant associations. The alumroot and wild bleeding heart in the garden shown here are both native to eastern North America.

You will find your native plant garden fits beautifully into your surroundings and needs very little maintenance. It also will be relatively free from pests and diseases, attract wildlife, and afford you long-lasting pleasure. 🌿

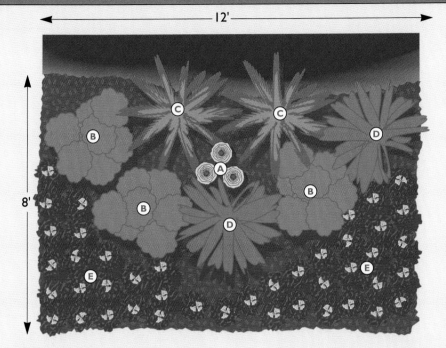

12'

8'

A. River birch, 1, 50 to 75 feet tall
B. Alumroot, 3, 2 to 3 feet tall
C. Christmas fern, 2, 2 to 3 feet tall
D. Grecian foxglove, 2, 3 feet tall
E. Wild bleeding heart, 43,
    12 to 18 inches tall
(See next page for more on plants.)

HERE'S HOW

STAKING A YOUNG TREE

1. Select your site and as soon as soil can be worked in the spring, measure off an 8 x 12-foot area. Remove sod and stones and till the soil 1 foot deep. Add 4 to 6 inches of organic compost and till again, 4 to 6 inches deep.

2. Dig a hole 8 to 12 inches wider than the rootball of a balled-and-burlapped river birch (A) 3 feet from the back and 4 feet from the left side of the garden. Make a small mound of soil in the bottom of the hole for roots. Remove plastic and metal; leave burlap around rootball. Plant so that the top of the rootball is level with soil surface.

3. Backfill the hole, tamping the soil every 6 inches and watering to remove air pockets. Stake tree to prevent it from blowing over until roots grow to anchor it (see Here's How, on this page).

4. Beginning in the back left corner, spacing everything 3 feet apart and planting at same depth as they were in their containers, plant 1 alumroot (B), 2 ferns (C), and 1 foxglove (D) across the back. Next, plant 1 alumroot on either side of the tree. Plant 1 foxglove in front of the tree.

5. Plant bleeding hearts (E) as shown, 1 foot apart, beginning at the left edge of garden coming forward. Continue as shown in the diagram above. Remember to stagger the plants for a more natural look.

6. Mulch the garden with organic material, and water well.

Drive two 6-foot stakes 18 inches into the soil on either side of tree. Cut old rubber hosing into two 1-foot sections. Thread guy wires through the two pieces of hose. Wrap one end of wire around top of one stake and around tree trunk at approximately the same height, with hose-covered wire against the tree. Wrap other end of wire around the same stake. Repeat on opposite side of the tree.

In areas of high wind, especially when planting in sandy soil, use three evenly spaced stakes. Remove stakes and wires the following spring.

Natural Choices for a Native Garden

Native and naturalized plants are hardy and non-invasive, often having attractive foliage even when not in bloom. Plant them in similar conditions and these plants will perform beautifully in your garden, where they also will attract native wildlife.

In their natural habitat, plants usually grow in mixed groups. You can replicate this natural look by staggering plant patterns and having plants mingle informally at the edge of groups.

Buy native plants from your local nursery since they rarely survive when dug up from the wild and digging them may be illegal. Choose plants that work together for an environmentally balanced garden. Here, ferns, alumroot, and the naturalized foxgloves will grow better during hot summer months under the dappled shade of the birch tree, and the bleeding heart will bloom all season. ❧

RIVER BIRCH
Betula nigra
50-75 feet tall x 30-50 feet wide
Zones 5-9
Catkins April to May; deciduous, oval, serrated foliage; silver-gray peeling bark, red-pink beneath; average, well-drained soil; full sun; medium to high water. Attracts wildlife.

ALUMROOT
Heuchera americana
2-3 feet tall
Zones 5-8
Greenish white flowers May to June; rosette of lobed, leaves, maroon-white when young; average to rich, well-drained soil; partial shade; medium to high water. Do not crowd.

WILD BLEEDING HEART (TURKEY CORN)
Dicentra eximia
12-18 inches tall
Zones 3-8
Pink, heart-shaped flowers March to frost; finely cut leaves; average to rich, well-drained soil, high organic matter; partial shade; medium to high water.

CHRISTMAS FERN
Polystichum acrostichoides
2-3 feet tall
Zones 3-10
Evergreen fronds (leaves), arching form; moist or wet soil, rich in organic matter; in South, plant in shade; in North, partial shade; high water. Cut fronds for use in flower arrangements.

GRECIAN FOXGLOVE
Digitalis lanata
30-36 inches tall
Zones 4-9
White, tubular flowers June to July; lance-shaped leaves; average to rich, well-drained soil, rich in organic matter; partial shade; medium to high water. Perennial or biennial.

CARE FOR YOUR NATIVE PLANT GARDEN

SPRING Remove boughs and excess mulch. Remove or cut back invasive, encroaching plants or any broken tree branches. Spread organic mulch around the base of plants to smother weeds.

SUMMER Water plants during hot, dry weather. Cut back flower stalks after flowering to prevent seed formation. Adding compost or other organic matter will help to retain moisture, keep the soil cool, and provide additional nutrients.

FALL Cut dead foliage and spread healthy trimmings around plants. Remove diseased foliage and discard away from the garden. Cover plants with light mulch, such as straw, that will not pack. Hold mulch in place with evergreen boughs. ❧

Alternative

A NATIVE SOUTHWEST GARDEN

A native garden in the Southwest is a gratifying way to meet challenging conditions. The hot, dry climate, compounded by sandy, often alkaline, soil, strong winds, and torrential, infrequent rains, has not deterred the adaptation of a host of strikingly beautiful plants that will help you create a dramatic landscape.

When choosing the plants for your garden, investigate the conditions in which each plant grows, including climate, soil, winds, and location. Then, to ensure success, find a site in your garden where conditions are similar.

You can expect your native plants to have a high survival rate and remain vigorous during the growing season with little care and maintenance. They require minimal water, and this means that not only the environment benefits but that you do, too, financially and with less work. In addition, these plants will provide both habitat and food for native animals. You may want to think of your native garden as one step toward the reestablishment of lost native territory. 🌿

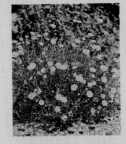

DESERT MARIGOLD
Baileya multiradiata
12-18 inches tall
Zones 8-10
Bright yellow, daisy-like flowers April to October that dry to a papery, pale yellow on the plant; gray-green, woolly foliage; average to poor, dry, well-drained, sandy soil; full sun; minimal water. Tolerates drought and intense heat. Beautiful form and color.

PINELEAF BEARD-TONGUE
Penstemon pinifolius
15-24 inches tall
Zones 5-10
Many scarlet, tubular flowers along upright stalks May to June, fewer through September; evergreen, lance-shaped, bright green foliage; poor, dry, well-drained, sandy soil; full sun or part shade; minimal water. Tolerates drought and intense heat. Very attractive to hummingbirds.

DESERT ZINNIA
Zinnia grandiflora
6-12 inches tall
Zones 5-10
Daisy-like yellow flowers with raised centers either red or green, June to October; wiry, grass-like, pale gray-green foliage; average to poor, dry, well-drained, sandy soil; full sun; minimal water. Tolerates drought and intense heat. Cultivar 'Acerosa' has white flowers.

BLUE PALO VERDE
Cercidium floridum
20-30 feet tall x 20-30 feet wide
Zones 6-10
Yellow flowers in spring or after rain; tiny, blue-green leaves in spring only, bare branches rest of the year; smooth, blue-green bark with spiny, green, twiggy branches; dry, sandy, well-drained soil; full sun; minimal water. Very tolerant of heat and drought including reflected heat from buildings. Attracts birds and small animals.

MEXICAN BUSH SAGE
Salvia leucantha
3-4 feet tall
Zones 9-10
Clump of arching stems tipped with long spikes of rosy purple bracts and small white flowers July to October; woolly, gray-green, lance-shaped leaves 1 to 3 inches long; average to poor, dry, well-drained, sandy soil; full sun/part shade; low water. Tolerates drought and intense heat.

A Wildlife Garden

THIS GARDEN THRIVES WITH

SUN
Full

WATER
Medium

SOIL
Average

Fragrant, brightly colored native flowers attract birds and insects to a wildlife garden. Most native flowers have abundant pollen and nectar, providing food for insects and birds. By encouraging insects, you will also increase the bird population visiting your garden, and insects will help to pollinate fruiting shrubs and trees nearby.

Locate your wildlife garden near trees and open fields where habitat will be available for the kind of wildlife you wish to attract. Plant flowers in the large drifts, or masses, that wildlife prefers, rather than in spotty plantings. Wildlife numbers will increase over the coming years, so plan to locate the garden where it is possible to expand its size, but make your first garden small and easy to care for.

Never use pesticides or insecticides in or near the wildlife garden. Even biologically engineered viruses, such as Bt which infects all caterpillars, can injure desirable wildlife. Chemical pesticides can drift or run off from other areas, killing plants and wildlife. Invest in a reliable resource to identify good and bad caterpillars and handpick them off rather than spray.

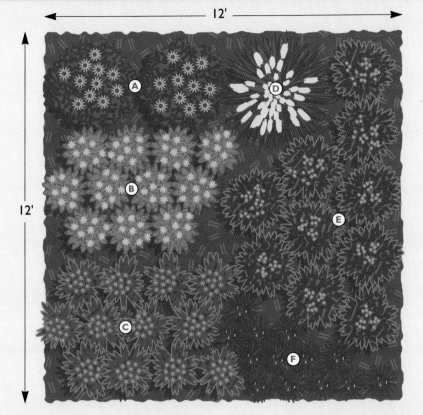

12'

12'

PLANT LIST

A. Black-eyed Susan, 2,
4 to 6 feet tall

B. Pincushion flower, 11,
2 to 2 ½ feet tall

C. Aster, 12, 2 to 3 feet tall

D. Eulalia grass, 1, 4 to 6 feet tall

E. Butterfly weed, 10, 2 feet tall

F. German flag, 13, 2 to 4 feet tall

(See next page for more on plants.)

1. Mark an area 12 x 12 feet and remove sod, till soil, add 3 to 4 inches of compost, and retill the soil.

2. Along the back, plant 2 black-eyed Susans (A).

3. Plant a row of 4 pincushion flowers (B) in front of the black-eyed Susans; then plant a second row of 4 pincushion flowers offset in front of the first row, and then a third row of 3 pincushion flowers offset in front of the second row. Space plants and rows 16 inches apart.

4. Plant 3 offset rows each of 4 asters (C) in front of the pincushion flowers, spacing plants and rows 16 inches apart.

5. At the garden back, 2 feet to the right of the black-eyed Susans, plant 1 eulalia grass (D).

6. Plant a row of 5 butterfly weeds (E) along the right side of the garden. To the left, plant 2 offset rows of butterfly weed, as shown.

7. Plant a row of 5 German flags (F) along the front on the right, and offset 3 rows behind it of 4, 3, and 1, as shown.

8. Mulch the garden and water all plants thoroughly until the garden is well established.

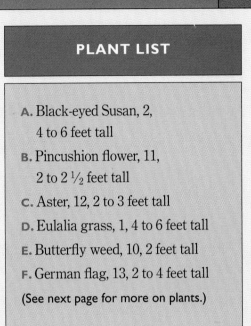

HERE'S HOW

BARREL PLANTING FOR WINTER BIRDSEED

Fill a half barrel with garden soil enriched with compost. Plant six common sunflower plants evenly spaced. Use a 3- to 6-foot variety, such as *Helianthus annuus* 'Velvet Tapestry' or 'Sunspot', which will set large flowers and seed heads on sturdy stems. In the fall, loosely tie individual stems together to keep them upright in the winter. Sunflower seeds are a favorite of winter songbirds.

Wildlife-Attracting Plants

To attract a wide variety of wildlife to your garden, choose plants that most resemble native ones. Native plants have coexisted with wildlife, providing food and habitat. Hybrid plants, varieties developed by breeders, are poor choices for your wildlife garden. Fragrance, pollen, nectar, and other characteristics that attract wildlife often are bred out of hybrids in favor of large, prolific flowers. Choose plants that either are specified as non-hybrids or listed as native plants.

The plants chosen here for your wildlife garden require full sun and well-drained soil. After spring, they do not need to be fertilized and will provide you with a sequence of blooms all season. Allow late flowers to produce seeds for birds during the fall and winter and for volunteer seedlings next spring. Clean water, available all year long, will also attract birds to your wildlife garden. ❧

BLACK-EYED SUSAN
Rudbeckia hirta
3 feet tall
Zones 4-9
Raised brown centers on golden, 3-inch, daisy-like flowers June to October; hairy leaves with distinct veins; average, well-drained soil; full sun; medium water. Long-lasting cut flower. Self-sows.

PINCUSHION FLOWER
Scabiosa caucasica
2-2 ½ feet tall
Zones 4-9
Blue, white, lavender, or pink, 2- to 3-inch, flat flowers June to October with extended stamens, wiry stems; leaves forming a low clump; average, well-drained soil; full/part sun; medium water.

ASTER
Aster x frikartii
2-3 feet tall
Zones 4-9
Purple, daisy-like, 2- to 3-inch, fragrant flowers July to September; coarse, deep green oval leaves; average, well-drained soil; full/part sun; medium water. Long-lasting flowers.

EULALIA GRASS (MAIDEN GRASS)
Miscanthus sinensis
4-6 feet tall
Zones 5-9
White or tan, feathery flowers 3 feet above clump of narrow, arching leaves last all winter; average, well-drained soil; full/part sun; medium water. Non-invasive. Attracts birds.

BUTTERFLY WEED
Asclepias syriaca
2 feet tall
Zones 4-9
Dusty pink, star-shaped flowers in flat terminal clusters July to August; lance-shaped leaves; poor to average, well-drained soil; full/part sun; low to medium water. Long taproot.

GERMAN FLAG (BEARDED IRIS)
Iris germanica
2-4 feet tall
Zones 4-9
Dark blue or violet, 4- to 6-inch, yellow-bearded flowers May to June; deep green, sword-shaped leaves; average, well-drained soil; full/part sun; medium water. Attracts insects and birds.

CARE FOR YOUR WILDLIFE GARDEN

SPRING Remove winter mulch and trim back any remaining dead plants. Cultivate soil between perennial plants, working in compost or fertilizer. If incorporating annuals, till areas, adding 3 to 4 inches of compost. After replanting, mulch entire garden. Provide water for birds.

SUMMER Water plants regularly, especially during hot weather. Remove faded blooms to prolong flowering. Toward the end of summer, allow flowers to go to seed. Keep clean water available for wildlife.

FALL Trim only perennials not producing seed heads to 3 to 4 inches. Remove annuals. Compost healthy plant materials. Mulch perennials for winter without knocking down seed stalks. Install a heater to prevent birdbath water from freezing during cold weather. ❧

Alternative

BUTTERFLY GARDEN

Few garden projects offer more summer enjoyment than a garden planned to attract butterflies. Butterflies can't be confined to one area but can be lured by flowers, and bright colors in drifts, or masses, will attract them. To encourage a variety of visitors, locate your butterfly garden near uncut weeds, naturalized areas, or open fields.

Different species of butterflies appear from early spring to fall and are fond of different plants. For example, swallowtails prefer thistles and monarch butterflies are attracted to milkweed. You will find special pleasure in providing a patch of plants that harbor a certain kind of butterfly, since it may well return to the same patch every year at the right time. Butterflies need to feed through all stages of their development, from caterpillar to adult, but the chance to watch them feed is worth sacrificing some foliage in your garden. They need the carbohydrates, since flight demands energy, and they need warmth, so plant in full sun.

By introducing natural landscape elements into your neighborhood, you will be making a valuable contribution to the ecosystem. Buying your native plants from nurseries rather than transplanting from the wild will help to preserve your local habitats. ❧

VERONICA
Veronica spicata **'Blue Carpet'**
12-15 inches tall
Zones 3-9
Bright blue, 3- to 6-inch flowers July to August; dense, oval, toothed, narrow, deep green leaves; average, well-drained soil; full/part sun; medium water. Remove faded flowers for continuous blooms. Good cut flower.

PAINTED DAISY
Chrysanthemum coccineum
2 feet tall
Zones 4-9
Pink, red, or white, 3-inch, daisy-like flowers on long stems June to July; finely cut, deep green, fern-like foliage forming a rounded clump; average, well-drained soil; full sun; medium water. Remove faded blossoms to extend flowering period. Good cut flower.

PURPLE FOXGLOVE
Digitalis x mertonensis
3-6 feet tall
Zones 4-9
Pinkish purple, tubular flowers along terminal stalks June to July; gray-green, hairy, oval leaves; average, moist soil; part sun/part shade; medium water. Tolerates more sun in cooler summer climates. Self-sows.

FRENCH MARIGOLD
Tagetes patula
10-14 inches tall
All zones
Golden yellow, 2-inch double flowers all summer; dense, finely cut, deep green, aromatic foliage; average, well-drained soil; full sun; medium water. Also orange, red, mahogany, or bicolor flowers 1 to 3 inches wide, single or double. Good cut flower. Annual.

ALUMROOT
Heuchera americana
2-3 feet tall
Zones 5-8
Greenish white, tubular flowers along 3-foot stalks May to June; rounded, lobed, green leaves with maroon and white markings when young form a 2-foot-tall rosette; average to rich, well-drained soil; part sun/part shade; medium to high water. Remove flower stalks to promote blooms.

An Informal Herb Garden

THIS GARDEN THRIVES WITH

SUN	WATER	SOIL
Full	Low	Poor

Herbs have been cultivated since the earliest civilizations, and for good reason. Herb gardens were vital components of everyday life, often depicted in manuscripts, drawings, and tapestries.

Today, growing your own herb garden can satisfy your personal interests whether they be herbal remedies, natural plant dyes, culinary pursuits, or, of course, garden design. Herbs provide a vast array of foliage colors and textures, flowers, and fragrances from which to choose. They have been planted in many styles, from casual kitchen gardens to formal, geometrical knot beds designed around monastic or Shakespearean themes. The garden shown at left features an array of herbs in a sunny, informal border.

Hardworking herbs often do double duty in annual and perennial beds, grown for both beauty and utility. They serve landscaping purposes as hedges (lavender, for instance) and are used as ground covers (sweet woodruff). They also make good companion plants in the vegetable garden. Herb flowers attract pollinators, such as bees and butterflies, and can help repel garden pests that prey on other plants. ❧

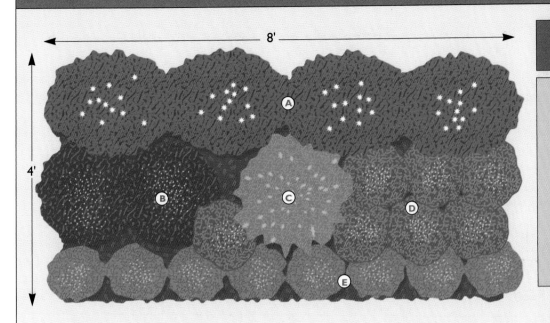

PLANT LIST

A. Feverfew, 4, 3 feet tall

B. Basil, 2, 2 feet tall

C. Sage, 1, 2 feet tall

D. Santolina, 7, 18 inches tall

E. Thyme, 8, 1 foot tall

(See next page for more on plants.)

1. Measure a 4 x 8-foot area and remove sod and stones. Till the soil to a depth of 1 foot. Spread 3 to 4 inches of compost over the garden surface and till again, 3 to 4 inches deep. Plant all herbs at the same depth they grew in their containers.

2. Beginning at the back left corner of the garden, plant the 4 feverfews (A) 2 feet apart across the back.

3. Returning to the left side, 2 feet in front of the feverfews, plant 2 basils (B) 18 inches apart. Plant 1 sage (C) 2 feet to the right of the basils.

4. Two feet to the right of the sage, plant 2 rows of 3 santolinas (D), each 1 foot apart. Plant the first row 14 inches in front of the feverfews. Stagger the second row 1 foot in front of the first. Plant the final santolina between the sage and basil as shown.

5. Plant 8 thymes (E) 1 foot apart along front edge of the garden.

6. Water plants well and mulch with 2 to 4 inches of compost.

HERE'S HOW

DRYING HERBS

Cut herbs in the morning after the dew has dried and just before they come into bloom. Remove any damaged leaves. Tie stems together in 1-inch-thick bunches with cotton string and hang upside down at least 6 inches apart in a warm, dry place out of direct sun. A dark, well-ventilated attic is ideal. In dusty areas, place herbs in a paper bag and secure the top. When crispy dry to the touch, package in airtight containers. Pack whole leaves when possible and crush just before use.

Herbs for Beauty and Interest

The herbs in this garden are steady, reliable performers with long traditions behind them. Feverfew, a profuse bloomer, was commonly used to lower fevers. Santolina's feathery gray foliage has a fresh, pine-like fragrance that has been used to repel insects. Feverfew, santolina, sage, and thyme all dry well, retaining their color. Sage, a popular seasoning, makes a flavorful tea considered good for colds and is sometimes used in hair rinses. Thyme has been used for everything imaginable, including mummification and snakebite. Today, it is used as a culinary seasoning or a decorative garden accent. Basil, perhaps the most popular of all herbs, has been an important cooking ingredient since antiquity. While, in general, herbs require very little maintenance, basil, sage, and thyme all need their blossoms removed to keep leaves more flavorful and aromatic. ❧

FEVERFEW
Chrysanthemum parthenium
2-3 feet tall
Zones 4-9
White, daisy-like flowers with yellow centers July to September; strongly aromatic, fern-like foliage; poor to average, well-drained soil; full sun; water only when dry. Repels insects. Self-sows.

BASIL
Ocimum basilicum
1-2 feet tall
All zones
Small, white, tubular flowers July to frost; aromatic leaves can be purple-tinged; slightly alkaline, rich, moist, well-drained soil; full sun; low water. Mulch after soil has fully warmed. Many varieties. Annual.

SAGE
Salvia officinalis
18-24 inches tall
Zones 4-8
Pink, purple, white, or blue tubular flowers in June; soft leaves on woody stems; average, well-drained soil; full sun; water only when dry. Benefits from organic matter in soil. Many varieties.

SANTOLINA (LAVENDER COTTON)
Santolina chamaecyparissus
18-24 inches tall
Zones 6-8
Small, bright yellow, button-shaped flowers June to July; fine, dense, aromatic, silver-gray, evergreen foliage; poor to average, alkaline, well-drained soil; full sun; low water.

THYME
Thymus vulgaris
12-15 inches tall
Zones 5-9
Scented clusters of white, pink, purple, or lavender flowers June to July; tiny leaves; poor to average, well-drained soil; full sun/partial shade; low water. Attracts bees.

CARE FOR YOUR HERB GARDEN

SPRING Remove winter protection and all debris from herb bed. Cultivate lightly to improve soil aeration and ability to hold water. Replace mulch, taking care to keep it several inches away from the crowns of the plants to prevent rot.

SUMMER Water in dry weather. Harvest leaves just before flowering for strongest flavor and fragrance. Remove flower buds to extend harvest. Mulch plants needing frequent watering and, after soil temperature rises, those needing warm soil.

FALL Harvest leaves and flowers before the first frost. After frost, remove annuals and compost healthy plants. Cut perennials back to 6 inches and cover with 4 to 6 inches of organic mulch. Cover with evergreen boughs to hold mulch for the winter. ❧

Alternative

NIGHT-SCENTED HERB GARDEN

Evening, when scent hangs in the moist air, is a great time to enjoy your herb garden. By placing your garden near a patio or an open window, you'll be able to enjoy its rich mixture of fragrances.

Informal herb gardens can provide plenty of space for your plant choices and allow you to harvest what you wish, when you wish. Be sure to plant groupings to avoid a confusing jumble of mixed plants. Single plants can be used for accent. Herbs that are large, bold, or have some other spectacular quality can be displayed to advantage against the background of plants in groups.

Most herbs have brittle roots that are sensitive to rough handling. When you transplant herbs into your garden, use care when removing them from their containers. Keep the rootball intact as much as possible and do not attempt to spread out the root system. Buying herb plants that are grown in single containers is a good idea.

These alternative plants grow well in either full sun or partial shade and will also show well at night. Most of the plants have light-colored foliage or flowers; their grays, whites, and silvers, when reflected in moonlight or artificial lighting, will create a peaceful and soothing atmosphere.

SOUTHERNWOOD
Artemisia abrotanum
3-5 feet tall
Zones 4-8
Tiny, light yellow flowers in August; aromatic, feathery, gray-green foliage on upright, woody stems; moist, poor to average, slightly alkaline, well-drained soil; full sun/part shade; low water. Mulch with organic matter. Repels moths.

SWEET CICELY
Myrrhis odorata
2-3 feet tall
Zones 3-7
Flat-topped, lacy, white clusters of flowers above foliage May to June; dense, shiny, fern-like leaves; moist, average to rich, well-drained soil; full sun/part shade; low water. Organic matter worked into soil is beneficial. Edible, anise-flavored leaves, seed pods and roots.

LEMON-SCENTED GERANIUM
Pelargonium crispum
1-2 feet tall
All zones
Rosy pink flowers all summer; deep green, finely cut foliage; moist, average to rich, well-drained soil; full sun/part shade; low water. Mulch with compost to increase blooms and deepen leaf color. Easy-to-root cuttings can be overwintered indoors for next year's garden.

GARDEN CHAMOMILE (ROMAN CHAMOMILE)
Chamaemelum nobile
9-12 inches tall
Zones 3-8
Small, white, daisy-like flowers with yellow centers all summer; lacy, apple-scented foliage on trailing stems; moist, average, well-drained soil; full sun/part shade; low water. Applying organic mulch reduces the need to water. Flowers and leaves used to make tea.

RUE
Ruta graveolens
18-36 inches tall
Zones 4-9
Yellow flowers all summer; aromatic, dense, blue-green foliage; poor to average, well-drained soil; full sun/part shade; low water. Foliage may irritate skin, so wear gloves when handling or working nearby.

A Tasteful Mixed Border

THIS GARDEN THRIVES WITH

SUN
Full

WATER
Medium

SOIL
Average

Mixed borders are gardens that contain shrubs, perennials, and annuals often located in front of a fence, wall, row of trees or other shrubs. They can be tucked into an area devoid of foliage and flowers or planted in front of a backdrop of shrubs or evergreens. The existing pieris shrub border in this garden, for example, has interest added by the colorful flowers planted in the semi-enclosure of the shrubs as well as all along the border front. Annual and perennial flowers, framed by the shiny, deep green pieris leaves, brighten the space and create additional interest in the planting.

Choose a design for your mixed border that will coordinate with existing plantings. The yard and garden surrounding this border are rather formal and so the symmetrical layout shown works well. If your yard has more random plantings, use a more informal, asymmetrical design. Also, keep your mixed border planting in scale with its surroundings. If your border fronts a row of large conifers, you may want to add a background grouping of shrubs so that small annuals don't look lost.

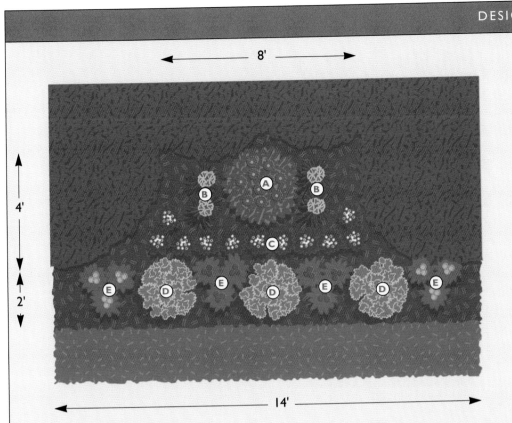

PLANT LIST

A. Zinnia, 1 red, 3 feet tall

B. Canna, 4 yellow, 5 feet tall

C. Cape marigold, 11, 1 foot tall

D. Variegated wintercreeper, 3,
4 to 5 feet tall

E. Geranium, 6 pink, 6 red,
10 inches tall

(See next page for more on plants.)

HERE'S HOW

CANNAS FOR INDOOR BLOOMS

Choose dwarf canna varieties for indoor blooms. In late winter or early spring, select a pot that has drainage holes and fill it to 3 inches from the top with a moisture-retentive potting mix. Place the rhizomes on the soil surface, then cover with 2 inches of soil mix. Place the pot in a bright, sunny window and keep rhizomes moist. After sprouting, continue to keep the soil moist.

1. Prepare an 8 x 4-foot area in front of shrubs or trees, with an additional 2- x 14-foot-long strip in front, by removing sod or other ground cover, tilling the soil, adding 2 inches of compost, and retilling.

2. At back of border, plant 1 zinnia (A) in the center.

3. Plant 2 cannas (B) on each side of the zinnia, one in front of the other.

4. Plant a row of 9 Cape marigolds (C) in front of the cannas and the zinnia, and 1 more offset behind each end of the row.

5. Plant 3 variegated wintercreepers (D) spaced 4 feet apart in front of the Cape marigolds.

6. Between the wintercreepers, plant 4 groups of 3 pink or red geraniums (E). Within each single-color trio, place 2 in the back and 1 offset in front.

7. Mulch your garden and water it thoroughly.

Perfect Plants for a Mixed Border

Plants in this mixed border need well-drained soil and full sun. Avoid locations on the north side of a planting or where shrubs may cast shadows for most of the day.

Choose plants with colorful foliage or blooms for use with a massed evergreen shrub planting in a small garden. Larger gardens can combine perennials, annuals, shrubs and small, ornamental trees for continuing color.

In this garden, the variegated wintercreeper foliage, both colorful and evergreen, will brighten the border throughout the year. Tall plants, such as cannas and zinnias, bring the smaller annuals, geraniums, and Cape marigolds into scale with the background pieris shrubs.

In cold climates, dig canna rhizomes after the first frost. Remove clinging soil and cut dead foliage to 1 to 3 inches. Allow the rhizomes to air dry for 12 hours. Store, covered with sand, in a location protected from freezing.

RED ZINNIA
Zinnia elegans 'Splendor Scarlet'
To 3 feet tall
All zones
Double, red flowers all summer; deep green, oval leaves; average, well-drained soil; full sun; medium water. Remove faded blossoms for continuous flowers. Give plants good air circulation.

YELLOW CANNA
Canna x *generalis* 'Yellow King Humbert'
4-5 feet tall
Zones 7-10
Yellow flowers with red spots in large, terminal clusters July to frost; deep green, lance-shaped leaves; moist, rich soil; full sun; medium/high water. Grown as an annual in cool climates.

CAPE MARIGOLD (AFRICAN DAISY)
Dimorphotheca sinuata
12-18 inches tall
All zones
Daisy-like, 1½-inch, pink, red, white, or purple flowers all summer; oval, deep green foliage; average, well-drained soil; full sun; medium water. Will self-sow. Flowers close at dark.

VARIEGATED WINTERCREEPER
Euonymus fortunei 'Emerald Gaiety'
4-5 feet tall
Zones 4-9
Insignificant blossoms; prized for its dense, evergreen leaves combining dark green and white; average, well-drained soil; full sun/partial shade; medium water.

GERANIUM
Pelargonium x *hortorum* 'Multibloom Scarlet' and 'Multibloom Pink'
8-10 inches tall
All zones
Numerous flower clusters all summer; rounded, lobed green leaves can be tinged with red; average, well-drained soil; full sun; medium water.

CARE FOR YOUR MIXED BORDER

SPRING Start the canna rhizomes indoors 6 to 10 weeks before planting time. In warm climates, plant directly outdoors. Cultivate soil for annual plantings and between immature shrubs, working compost into soil.

SUMMER Remove faded flowers from annuals regularly to encourage continuous blooms. Water the garden thoroughly during hot, dry weather. Spread a layer of organic mulch to control the weeds and to retain moisture.

FALL Dig up and pot your Cape marigolds for indoor flowers. After frost, remove dead plants, compost healthy ones. Dig and prepare canna rhizomes for storage. Mulch young shrubs and perennials to winter-protect roots.

Alternative

A SHADE-LOVING BORDER WITH YEAR-ROUND INTEREST

In shady locations, annuals, perennials, and shrubs can create an exciting mixed border that will be attractive all year. Shrubs and flowering plants provide winter interest with the color or shapes of stems and twigs, as well as with dried flowers, seed pods, or fruits. In addition, these plants usually attract wildlife during the cold months. For example, red osier dogwoods are native plants with bright-colored twigs and white berries that attract songbirds during the winter.

Be sure to provide these shade-loving plants with plenty of water. To retain moisture, add compost generously when preparing the soil and mulch the garden heavily during the growing season. A mixed border of annuals, perennials, and shrubs requiring a high amount of water should not be placed near plants needing very well-drained or dry soil. Look for a location where required conditions are comparable.

In dark, shaded borders, use annuals or plants with brightly colored foliage for all-season interest. Annuals that bloom profusely in the shade, such as wishbone flower and monkey flower, can add summer color with their unique, attention-getting flowers. 🐾

ROCKET LARKSPUR (ANNUAL LARKSPUR)
Consolida ambigua **'Imperial Blue Bell'**
3-4 feet tall
All zones
Deep blue, double flowers in June, numerous upright clusters per plant; dark green, hairy, deeply cut foliage; average to rich, moist, well-drained soil; part sun/part shade; medium to high water. Long-lasting cut flower. Annual. Self-sows.

RED OSIER DOGWOOD
Cornus sericea **'Isanti'**
2-3 feet tall
Zones 2-8
Small, whitish flowers June to July in flat clusters; green leaves with distinct veins, purplish red in fall; poor to rich, moist soil; part sun/part shade; medium to high water. Brilliant red stems in winter. Native plant. Attracts wildlife.

WISHBONE FLOWER
Torenia fournieri **'Happy Faces'**
6-8 inches tall
All zones
Tubular flowers all summer with white throats, opening with overlapping blue or pink petals having darker splotches; deep green, spreading foliage; average to rich, moist soil; part sun/full shade; medium to high water. Dig up and bring indoors for winter blooms.

MONKEY FLOWER
Mimulus x hybridus
12-18 inches tall
All zones
Red, yellow, and pink, trumpet-shaped flowers all summer, sometimes with spots; dense, green leaves; average to rich, moist soil; part/full shade; medium to high water. Keep constantly moist and remove faded blossoms for continuous flowering.

Adding Accents for Design

A SIMPLE TRELLIS

Trellises are upright structures that can support climbing vines and will provide an attractive focal point in your garden even when standing alone. A trellis can also be used to create shade and to separate one kind of garden space from another.

Trellises come in a variety of shapes, sizes, and materials. Use the overall character of your garden, the desired plant, or a specific location to help you choose a trellis style. Vase-shaped trellises are appropriate for climbing roses, for example, because the canes can be easily trained to grow along the fan-shaped form. Rectangular trellises provide a wide base for climbing annuals, such as morning glories. An overhead arch will frame the entrance to your yard or gardens, as well as create a tranquil nook for rest or reading.

The amount of maintenance required by your trellis will depend on the material used. Common trellis materials include fiberglass, plastic, wood, and metal. Fiberglass and plastic require little in the way of care and maintenance. Natural wood, depending on the finish, may need only simple maintenance or repair. Painted trellises will have to be sanded and repainted every few years to keep them looking their best.

Once you have your trellis, position it where the vines you plant will receive proper sunlight. Unless your plant needs shade, place the trellis to the plant's north side. 🌣

HAVE ON HAND:

▶ Trellis

▶ Tape measure

▶ Wooden mallet

▶ Stakes

▶ Wrench or pliers

Place two stakes on the north side of the planting area, the same distance apart as the trellis supports.

Replace stakes with trellis anchors. Check distance apart; sink anchors until 6 inches remain above ground.

Slide side supports into anchor bases and secure with supplied hardware. Tighten. Check stability.

Plant climbing plant(s) on south side of trellis and 12 to 18 inches from base for ease of maintenance.

A BEAUTIFUL BIRDBATH

A birdbath can act as a focal point in your garden while attracting beneficial birds to your yard. Place it in a sunny, open location near trees or shrubs, birdfeeders, or plants with berries or seed pods so birds can watch for predators, seek refuge, and find food all in one area.

A birdbath located near a water faucet or convenient to a hose will enable you to provide clean, fresh water all year round. You can announce its availability by letting a hose drip into the birdbath or by purchasing an aerator to splash water. You can also use the mist setting on a hose nozzle as a bird shower. If you do this every day at the same time, birds will appear specifically for this special treat.

There are some things to consider before and after you buy your birdbath. Pedestals should be no less than 3 feet high to protect birds from predators. The basin should be shallow since most birds don't like deep water. And, if you're contemplating a one-piece birdbath, take into account that a two-piece model will be easier to empty.

You may want to buy a submersible water heater to keep your birdbath from freezing in winter. Never introduce chemicals to keep the water from freezing or to kill algae; birds could be harmed as well. Spraying or using chemicals nearby can also be toxic to birds. 🐦

HAVE ON HAND:

- ▶ Birdbath
- ▶ Tape measure
- ▶ Scissors
- ▶ Stake and string
- ▶ Lime for marking
- ▶ Shovel
- ▶ Decorative gravel
- ▶ Metal garden rake

Cut string to ¹/₂ basin diameter plus 1 foot. Drive stake into center of area; attach string; mark circle.

Use a shovel to remove sod and excavate the soil to a depth of 4 inches, keeping bottom even.

Fill depression with gravel. Tamp with rake to remove air pockets and to settle soil and gravel.

Rake the gravel until level. Measure to center of circle, place birdbath, and check level again before filling.

Glossary

ACCENTS features providing focal points, shape, or shade to garden design.

ACID (ACIDIC) SOIL soil with a pH lower than 7.0; acceptable for most plants; also known as a sour soil; the opposite of alkaline.

ALKALINE SOIL soil with a pH higher than 7.0; also know as a sweet soil; opposite of acid.

ANALOGOUS COLORS colors that appear side by side on the color wheel, such as red and purple.

ANNUALS plants that sprout from seed; grow, flower, set seeds, and die within one growing season.

AROMATIC HERBS grown for fragrance and utility; used in cooking and herbal teas; they can also be dried for decorative purposes.

ASPARAGUS FORK a tool whose 12- to 18-inch metal shank is often used for root-pruning and for removing weeds with long taproots.

BARE-ROOT PLANTS no soil around plant roots; they are usually shipped dormant. Many trees, shrubs, and perennials are sold this way, especially through mail-order catalogs.

BIENNIALS plants with a two-year life cycle. They produce leaves their first season; flower and set seed in their second season.

BONE MEAL finely ground white or light gray, rendered slaughterhouse bones; adds nitrogen and phosphorous to soil.

BROAD-LEAVED EVERGREENS nonconiferous shrubs or trees, such as rhododendrons or hollies, which retain green foliage year round.

BUILDER'S SAND also known as horticultural sand; has coarse, large grains that increase drainage and aeration when added to heavy soils.

BULB PLANTER a cylindrical, hand-held tool used to dig holes for bulbs; minimizes disturbance to nearby tree or shrub roots.

CANES stems; often used in relation to roses.

CANOPY the leafy upper branches of a tree.

CLAY SOIL soil composed of very small, flat particles that tend to pack together tightly; turns hard when dry; drains poorly without organic amendments.

CLIMBING ROSES roses that produce long stems that can be trained to climb a support.

COMPOST organic material composed of decaying plant and animal materials.

COTTAGE GARDEN an informal combination of annuals, shrubs, perennials, herbs and/or vegetables; originally a family garden of medicinal and culinary plants.

CROWN the point where roots join the above-ground parts of a plant.

CUTTINGS pieces of stems, leaves, or roots taken from plants for propagation.

DIVIDING the technique of separating a plant clump into several smaller parts.

DORMANT plants that are in a resting state, usually during a period of low or high temperatures. They may die down to the roots.

DOUBLE DIGGING the process of loosening the top 12 to 16 inches of soil by removing the top layer with a spade or shovel, loosening the lower layer with a spading fork, mixing in amendments, and replacing the top layer.

EDGING a line that establishes visual interest and separation; for example, between a lawn and the foliage of a shrub or perennial border.

FOLIAGE PLANTS annuals or perennials grown for leaf shape, size, texture, and color; supplying contrast and interest in the garden.

FORCING providing the right combination of temperatures to encourage growth and flowering; often used for growing flowering bulbs indoors.

GREEN MANURE cover crops such as buckwheat and annual ryegrass grown in the garden in fall and turned under in spring to enrich soil.

HARDY PLANTS plants in a given area that survive winter either in a dormant state or while holding green leaves. Hardiness can be affected by heat, rainfall, and other conditions.

HYBRIDS the offspring from genetically different parent plants. Resistant to pests and diseases, often more vigorous and productive than either parent; seeds produced often show characteristics of parents rather than the hybrid.

INFORMAL BORDERS characterized by curved lines, nongeometric planting patterns, and use of plants in their natural shapes.

ISLAND BEDS focal point plantings surrounded by lawn, paths or paving. Plants often set from tallest in center to shortest at edges for maximum visibility.

KNOT GARDEN a garden design that creates the illusion of entwined fabric or knotted rope.

LAYERING the process of treating a shoot so it will form roots while still attached to the parent plant; a common method of propagating roses.

LEACHING the loss of nutrients from the soil's top layer due to water draining through it.

MINIATURE WETLANDS areas in any garden where water is naturally retained and can be developed to support moisture-loving plants.

MULCH any material spread over the soil surface to retain soil moisture, moderate soil temperature, and suppress the growth of weeds.

NATIVE PLANTS species occurring naturally in any region; they are commonly hardy and easy-care.

NATURALIZE to plant randomly to create a natural effect, then let plants increase in number.

NEUTRAL PLANTS these often have gray or gray-green foliage. Used to offset color clashes, bridge visual gaps between textures, or to impart a feeling of spaciousness.

ORGANIC MATTER mulch or other material derived from decomposed plant or animal products.

PERENNIALS species that can live for more than two years.

PERGOLA an arbor or trellis connected with an open roof; used to support vines.

PERLITE white granules of a treated volcanic mineral; add to potting soil to improve drainage.

pH a measure of a soil's acidity or alkalinity on a scale of 1.0 to 14.0, with 7.0 neutral. A pH below 7.0 is acidic; above 7.0 is alkaline.

PINCHING removing a shoot tip using thumb and forefinger; encourages bushier growth.

PLANT FORM characteristic shape and size.

ROOTBALL the mass of roots and potting soil visible when you remove a plant from its pot.

SCALE overall size of a garden; helps determine the plants used in garden design.

SEED HEADS pods or clusters of seeds at the top of mature plants at the end of growing season.

SELF-SEEDING (SELF-SOWING) an annual's ability to drop seeds that successfully germinate and grow into seedlings.

SIMPLE DIGGING the process of loosening the top 1 foot of soil and amending it; suitable for shallow-rooted shrubs and perennials.

SOAKER HOSES porous, rubber hoses that allow seepage for deep root watering, eliminate evaporation and keep leaves dry.

SPECIMEN PLANT one plant set to highlight its full development; often a focal point.

STAGGERED PLANTING positioning plants so that one is not directly in front of another.

STAKING supporting tall plants with stakes to help keep them upright.

TEXTURE the surface characteristic of a plant.

TERMINAL STEM growing tip on a plant or shrub.

TRELLISES frames of varying shapes and sizes used to support climbing vines or canes.

VARIEGATED LEAVES foliage with discrete markings or margins.

VERMICULITE a lightweight, flaky, treated amendment that improves soil drainage.

WINTER GARDENS without flowers, depend on foliage, form and arrangement for interest.

Index

TIME-LIFE BOOKS IS A DIVISION OF TIME LIFE INC.

TIME-LIFE CUSTOM PUBLISHING

Vice President and Publisher	Terry Newell
Associate Publisher	Teresa Hartnett
Project Manager	Jennifer Pearce
Consulting Editor	Linda B. Bellamy
Director of Sales	Neil Levin
Director of Special Sales	Liz Ziehl
Director of New Product Development	Regina Hall
Managing Editor	Donia Ann Steele
Production Manager	Carolyn Mills Bounds
Quality Assurance Manager	Miriam P. Newton

Produced by Storey Communications, Inc.
Pownal, Vermont

President	M. John Storey
Executive Vice President	Martha M. Storey
Vice President and Publisher	Pamela B. Art
Director of Custom Publishing	Amanda Haar
Project Manager	Vivienne Jaffe
Book Design	Jonathon Nix/Verso Design
Design and Layout	Mark Tomasi
Design Assistant	Jennifer Jepson
Editing	Joan Burns
Author	Luanne Urfer
Primary Photography	Kevin Kennefick
Photo Styling	Kevin Kennefick and Derek Fell

Additional photography: Henry W. Art; Rich Baer; Cathy Wilkinson Barash; Dick Canby/PI; ©Crandall & Crandall; R. Todd Davis; Alan and Linda Detrick; Thomas Eltzroth; Derek Fell; Peggy Fisher; A. Blake Gardner; Harry Haralambou/PI; Margaret Hensel/PI; Bill Johnson; Charles Mann; Grace Maubach; J. Paul Moore; Karin O'Connor; Jerry Pavia; Pam Peirce; Kathleen Persoff; Paul Rocheleau; Richard Shiell; Pam Spaulding/PI; Joseph G. Strauch, Jr.; Patricia Taylor; Michael S. Thompson; Robert Walsh; Chuck Weight; judywhite.

© 1997 Time Life Inc. All rights reserved.
No part of this book may be reproduced in any form or by any electronic or mechanical means, including information storage and retrieval devices or systems, without prior written permission from the publisher, except that brief passages may be quoted for reviews.
First printing.
Printed in U.S.A.
TIME-LIFE is a trademark of Time Warner Inc. U.S.A.
Time-Life How-To is a trademark of Time-Life Books.

Library of Congress Cataloging-in-Publication Data
Time-Life how-to garden designs : simple steps to beautiful flower gardens.
        p.   cm.
Includes index.
ISBN 0-7835-4866-4
1. Gardens—Design. 2. Flower gardening.   I. Time-Life Books
Sb473.T56 1997
635.9—dc20   96-34319
                                                                              CIP

Books produced by Time-Life Custom Publishing are available at special bulk discount for promotional and premium use. Custom adaptations can also be created to meet your specific marketing goals. Call 1-800-323-5255.

Zone Map

ALASKA

HAWAII

Range of Average Annual Minimum
Temperatures for Each Zone

Zone 1	Below -50° F
Zone 2	-50° to -40° F
Zone 3	-40° to -30° F
Zone 4	-30° to -20° F
Zone 5	-20° to -10° F
Zone 6	-10° to 0° F
Zone 7	10° to 20° F
Zone 8	20° to 30° F
Zone 9	30° to 40° F
Zone 10	40° to 50° F
Zone 11	50° to 60° F